When the Water Run ... (and I loved it). The ... reader along apace. ... ing people we really care about. The saga of this warm and loving family living together in harmony in the wilderness above the Arctic Circle with only Eskimos and gold miners for neighbors is enthralling. To me it is the Little House on the Tundra!

—Dr. Pamelia S. Cromer
Educator

When the Water Runs is a poignant, informative view of life on the Alaskan frontier. This first-person account draws the reader into the stories of family love and laughter in the midst of the hardships of life. Once I started to read, I didn't want to stop!

—Elizabeth Sherrer
Literacy Consultant and Writer

This fascinating story of a remarkable pioneer family that found joy while enduring the hardships in the Alaskan frontier brought forth both tears and laughter as I walked through the pages of their adventures.

—Susan Gladhill
Educator

While I'm very grateful to be living with indoor plumbing and many of the "finer" things in life, reading this book has made the adventurer in me long to be able to visit the days of Audrey's youth and run across the tundra with her and her sisters and brother in the wild Alaska of old.

—Pat Cathey
Retired administrator, Fairbanks School District

WHEN THE
WATER RUNS

To John ~
Enjoy!
Cheryl Schuermann

WHEN THE
WATER RUNS
GROWING UP WITH ALASKA

CHERYL SCHUERMANN

Tate Publishing & *Enterprises*

Published by Tate Publishing & Enterprises, LLC
127 E. Trade Center Terrace | Mustang, Oklahoma 73064 USA
1.888.361.9473 | www.tatepublishing.com

Tate Publishing is committed to excellence in the publishing industry. The company reflects the philosophy established by the founders, based on Psalm 68:11,
"The Lord gave the word and great was the company of those who published it."

Book design copyright © 2007 by Tate Publishing, LLC. All rights reserved.
Illustration by Rick Fry
Cover design by Luke Southern
Interior design by Leah LeFlore

Published in the United States of America

ISBN: 978-1-60462-273-7
1. Biography: Personal Memoir 2. Regional: United States: Pacific
07.11.05

DEDICATION

To my mother, Audrey, and her remarkable family

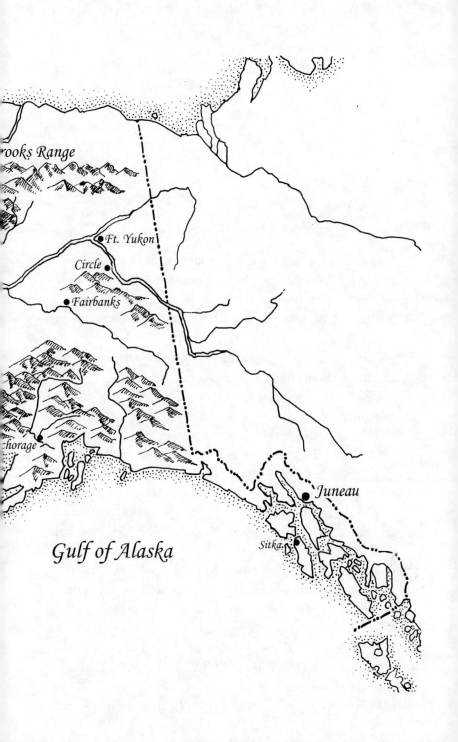

ACKNOWLEDGMENTS

FIRST OF ALL, I MUST THANK MY MOTHER, AUDREY DAVINE Purkeypile Wilcox, who provided me with so many wonderful recollections of her childhood and never tired of my endless questions and clarifications. I have cherished our many long conversations. Many thanks to my father, John Wilcox, who has provided continual encouragement and is as proud of his wife as any man could possibly be.

I wish to thank my family members who have always recognized the richness of their heritage and have been so supportive through this process: My brothers and sisters-in-law, Allen and Connie, Gary and Angie, and Todd and Carol collected and scanned photographs and called often to encourage me. I am grateful to my cousins, Ellen Anderson and Marilyn Anderson, who provided photographs and encouragement. Ellen's words, "Go, girl!" were the impetus I needed to tackle this project. My children, sons and daughters-in-law, David and Emily, Matthew and Tana, Andrew and Leslie, and Daniel and Marcy have been so very patient with a mom who has been distracted for many months. Through this process, my husband, Stan, has helped me to remain focused and has provided insight and wisdom. And I must thank and honor Irus and Sara Purkeypile for the lessons they have taught all of us.

Thank you to Artist Rick Fry for creating the map of the

state of Alaska. I am grateful to Alma Harwell Matlock, who many years ago recognized the significant contributions of my grandparents to the people of Alaska. In her book, *Teaching Above the Arctic Circle,* she recorded the highlights of their years as U.S. Government teachers in Selawik. During my research of the history of mining in the Ruby-Poorman mining district, Sharon Wilson at the Bureau of Land Management in Anchorage was helpful in providing information that clarified my grandfather's involvement with mining in that area.

TABLE OF CONTENTS

FOREWORD

MY MOTHER, AUDREY DAVINE PURKEYPILE WILCOX, WAS born in 1927 in Candle, Alaska. The daughter of Alaskan pioneers, she spent the first thirteen years of her life living among the native Eskimos and the non-native miners, trappers, and traders who came to take from the land. Her parents each arrived in Alaska at a time when the territory was viewed as a vast extension to the American frontier and a virtual goldmine of natural resources. Their lives were defined not by the accumulation of material wealth, but by their endurance and their dedication to the people they served. My mother delights in recalling her unique childhood and seldom misses an opportunity to share her memories with anyone who asks.

From a very early age, I was aware that my mother grew up in Alaska. I tried to imagine what her life in the North Country must have been like. The times that she showed me her treasures—gold nuggets, a small beaded Eskimo purse, one of her dolls—awakened in me an interest in her childhood. She often reminisced with me, sharing stories of her adventures with family and Eskimo friends. Her walking-to-school-in-the-snow story was not the standard parent talk aimed at unappreciative children—she truly did walk one and a half miles to school in the snow in forty-below-zero temperatures. (However, I have been able to verify that it was not uphill both ways.) Her childhood was filled with experiences that most children today would envy—riding on dog sleds, visiting Eskimo fish camps, panning gold, cross-country skiing, flying with bush pilots, and traveling down the Selawik River in a houseboat. During the 1920s and 30s, my mother and her siblings observed their parents' remark-able work among the Alaskan people and their commitment to building the Territory of Alaska.

In 1867, the United States purchased Alaska from Rus-sia and, in 1912, declared the North Country to be an offi-cial territory. The U.S. Government committed funds and resources for the purpose of developing this vast country and, subsequently, numerous programs were created and instituted. The territory was opened up for an extensive array of mining enterprises. A network of communication, includ-ing postal service and telegraph, began to emerge, even in the most remote areas. These services brought the Alaskans closer, not only to each other, but to "the lower forty-eight." The task of educating the indigenous people was a territorial priority and began to take shape as teachers were contracted and assigned to the remote districts. Some came responding to a calling and some came simply seeking adventure, yet both groups encountered the wonder and beauty of Alaska as well as its unforgiving harshness.

Itinerant doctors and nurses provided much-needed health services, including inoculation programs to stave off epidemics; however, the first responders in remote areas were usually willing, government-appointed health officers with limited training. To survive, the native population needed sustainable sources for food. The Department of the Interior introduced reindeer from Siberia, a bold plan involving not only the introduction of a new species to the area, but train-ing men who had only known hunting to be herdsmen.

My mother grew up in this era of Alaskan history. Her

parents, Irus and Sara Purkeypile, contributed to the growth of the territory in their official roles as postmaster, teacher, health officer, and reindeer superintendent. In these roles, they were front-line generals, regularly reporting to the government concerning not only the progress, but also the problems with these programs. Less official, but no less important, they were among those who settled in Alaska, raising their family and devoting their lives to the territory and its people.

During her years in Alaska, my grandmother, Sara Purkeypile, endured the darkness and cold of the winter months, anticipating the time when the long stretches of sunless days, bitter temperatures, and dwindling supplies gave way to light and warmth. The return of the sun meant the ice on the rivers and streams would break up and boats could run freely. Boats meant travel, and travel meant family fun and a refreshing reprieve from the heavy responsibilities in the Eskimo village. Ocean travel resumed, and much-needed supplies could be delivered. My grandmother referred to this time of year as the time "when the water runs."

Many of my grandmother's letters written to a cousin in New Jersey have proven valuable in understanding life in northern Alaska; several excerpts have been woven into this narrative. In 1967, my grandfather began writing his autobiography; although unfinished, his writings have given me insight into his journey to Alaska and the history of the Purkeypile family.

During the writing process, I sought to find my mother's voice in order to effectively share her memories. This book is written in first person, as if Audrey were sitting in your living room, talking about her childhood and her family over a cup of hot tea.

Enjoy.

INTRODUCTION

IT HAPPENS EVERY TIME. WHEN I TELL SOMEONE THAT I was born in northern Alaska, the barrage of questions begins. Most people find it difficult to imagine the harsh conditions that were my family's way of life for my entire childhood. These people are intrigued and always ask, "Audrey, what were your parents *doing* up there?" or "How in the world did you keep from *freezing* to death?"

My story can only begin with my parents. Two lives on different paths came together in this most unlikely place: Candle, Alaska. The small mining town would be the location of my birth several years later. My mother's desire to serve and better the lives of people led her to pursue the mission field. My father was also passionate, but he was driven by the desire to find wealth in the mines and gold fields of this new territory. This desire never left him and was never completely quieted, but what happened along the way were the experiences we call "life." My father, in his relentless pursuits, discovered not what he set out to find, but that which made him a very wealthy man.

As a child, I thought my life in Alaska was "normal." Wasn't this how everyone lived? My siblings and I were having so much fun that we would have been puzzled if anyone had suggested we were experiencing hardships. We would have wondered why everyone would not want to live like we did. This, I now realize, is a tribute to our parents. In 1967, my father began writing his autobiography. Although he did not complete this task, the recollections of his early life gave me insight into who he was and what inspired him. Several years ago, I obtained copies of letters that my mother wrote to her cousin Alice in New Jersey. Although these two cousins never met in person, they wrote faithfully to each other for forty years. These letters have been a window into my mother's life, the hardships she endured, and the grace with which she lived.

My parents were true pioneers and proud to be called "sourdoughs," the title given to men and women who "made it" in this spectacular North Country. As Alaskan pioneers, my parents learned to cope with adversity and hardship. They were strong, responsible, and rugged. Growing up, I learned to handle difficult situations because we lived to survive. The Eskimos, miners, trappers, and the Purkeypiles all shared a similar experience in enduring the harsh elements of northern Alaska.

What defines a rich existence? At the age of eighty, I have had ample opportunity to reflect on my life, the decisions made, and the paths taken. Where we are born, whom we encounter, the experiences we share with others, our personal relationships—how do they shape who we are as adults? In part, the place—the wild, untamed country of Alaska—shaped who I am today, but not nearly as much as the unique experiences and the people encountered during that magical time of childhood. I will always love Alaska. When I step onto Alaskan soil, I am home.

PARENTS

In 1904, I left Seattle for Nome to make a fortune; found not much gold, but a wife and later five children—gosh—struck it rich after all, I guess.

—Irus W. Purkeypile

Winter of 1918–19, Candle, Alaska

DAD NEVER TIRED OF TELLING ME HOW HE FIRST NOTICED her when she entered the room—and how his life was never again the same.

"Hey, Joe. Is that your sister? You gonna introduce me?"

"No way, Irus. She's not your type—and she's on her way to China. Sara is a missionary and only came to Candle to visit *me* before she leaves. Besides, she would never be interested in an old miner like you!"

But my dad did meet her that day. He was thirty-five years old at the time and had been focused on finding gold in the unforgiving North Country for nearly fifteen years. He had remained unmarried, perhaps not even thinking about a wife, or perhaps not finding the one perfect for him. Who had time for courting? Just surviving took all of one's energy and time. Dad never expected to meet someone like Mom in Alaska. A full six feet tall, he looked down at this pretty, petite woman as she extended her hand. Maybe his fortunes were changing.

During the dark winters in Candle, Alaska, when temperatures often fell to fifty below zero and blizzards were common, mining was nearly impossible. With nothing else to do, the miners gathered to enjoy conversation, food, and drink together. Dances were frequent, but with the scarcity of women in Candle, most men danced without the pleasure of a female partner. It was during this Candle "Social Season" of 1918–19 that my parents met and fell in love.

In my dad's autobiography, he referred to Mom as a "charming young Methodist deaconess," although she was thirty years old at the time, many years past the average marrying age for women in 1919. My parents were defined by different goals, dreams, education, and talents, but Mom set aside her plans to go to China. My parents became engaged and made arrangements to travel "outside" to Seattle to be married and enjoy a honeymoon. They traveled to Nome, where they would board a ship for Washington, but when they arrived at the dock on October 5, 1919, Dad received some unwelcome news. Dad recalled Mom's response.

"What? Irus—only one stateroom? How can that be?" Dad then told the ticket agent, "We will take the stateroom, but we will have to be married first." Fortunately, a local judge was available, and my parents said their vows in his apartment that afternoon.

Friends in Nome witnessed the ceremony—government teachers who would later tell my parents about the teaching opportunity in a remote Eskimo village. This friendship would ultimately determine my childhood experiences. The friends gave my parents their only wedding gift—a silver pickle fork and olive spoon with a "P" engraved on the handles. Though not at all practical for their new life of adventure, this gift was, nevertheless, cherished.

Not only do people ask me what my parents were doing in Alaska, but they often ask, "Why did they go there?"

Like many during the late 1800s, *their* parents were part of the great western migration. My dad was born in 1883 in Michigan to David and Amanda Purkeypile. His father had enlisted during Lincoln's second call for Union volunteers in 1861, serving until the end of the war in 1865. During this time, he fought in such battles as Gettysburg, Lookout Mountain, Missionary Ridge, the Second Bull Run, and Sherman's March to the Sea.

Irus and Sara Purkeypile leave Nome for honeymoon in Seattle on "Old Cordova" in 1919.

Most young men, after the work of war was done, began to think of adventure and dream of wealth. In 1886, my grandfather moved his wife and five sons west to Lincoln County, Nebraska, and lived in a dugout while building their sod house near the town of Wallace. The cry of "Gold!" and the lure of possible riches reached the Purkeypile men. One by one, the older sons moved farther west to seek their fortunes. In 1893, my grandfather continued west also, taking my dad with him to Washington. Dad attended school in Seattle, dropping out in the ninth grade due to illness. He did not return to school, but stayed in Seattle, working various jobs. Several years later, after becoming engaged, he decided to go to Alaska and stake a "marriage" claim; he hoped to strike it rich and provide a way to support his new bride and future family. Dad's fiancée was not enamored with the idea of living in Alaska, so he made the decision to go on ahead without her. He left for Nome in 1904 on the *Olympia*, a ninety-foot steamer.

Lacking a source of income, my dad immediately began cooking for the miners in the mining camps around Nome. When not working, he was following leads of gold, prospecting, and staking claims. At this time in Alaska, "prospecting" meant taking shovel and pan in hand to any promising stream or gravel bar. Always an entrepreneur, Dad opened a restaurant in Nome in 1905 and hired a French chef. The large menu, French food, and high prices were not popular with the miners, and Dad was forced to sell. In his autobiography, he wrote, "Just two months after the beginning of my great enterprise, I walked out with barely the shirt on my back. My prices for these fine French dishes were quite high. The fellow who took it over made it into the most successful restaurant in town. He served good American food at reasonable prices." For the next several years, Dad continued working as a cook in mining camps and prospecting gold, living in and around the new boomtowns of Solomon, Deering, Nome, and Candle.

My mother, Sara Whitehead, was born in Corning, Ohio, in 1888. When she was a young girl, her mother, Ida, developed tuberculosis. My grandfather, Matthew Whitehead, moved the family to Leadville, Colorado, to provide his wife with fresh air and healing. In spite of the move, Ida did not recover and died when my mom was eight years old. My grandfather moved close to relatives in British Columbia, taking some of the children, including Mom.

An educated woman, Mom completed two years of college in Toronto, focusing on missionary training. She was also trained as a midwife and was appointed a deaconess in the Methodist church. Driven by the desire to help people in need, Mom decided to travel to China and work as a Methodist missionary. Prior to making final preparations for her journey to China, Mom worked with wayward youth in Victoria, British Columbia. She also planned a trip to visit her younger brother, Joe, who was prospecting for gold in Candle, Alaska. Here is where my parents' paths crossed.

Originally intending only to winter on "the outside" before returning to Alaska, my parents stayed in Tacoma, Washington, for several years, where they bought a small chicken farm and started their family. Muriel (Mimi) was born in 1920, Norma in 1922, and June in 1924. When Mimi was one year old, my mom gave birth to a son, Irus, Jr., but he was with them only a precious short time. He died before he was three weeks old. My mom often referred to this time as a period of great sadness, "one of the milestones of life."

Irus and daughters on the chicken farm in Tacoma, about 1924.

Life continued and Dad had to work hard to support his young family. Besides operating the farm, he worked a number of odd jobs to make ends meet, sometimes only making one dollar per day. Dad was restless in Washington. His years of prospecting in Alaska were not very profitable, but they were far more exciting and promising than working for the railroad, barely making enough money to feed his young family.

The turning point came when the owner of the mining company in Candle telegraphed Dad, asking him to return and work in the mines. Dad had proven himself an expert in some aspects of mining, and he found the opportunity to return to Alaska irresistible; he decided to move his family to Candle. He had spent several years working in mines around Candle, so for him, this move seemed like going home.

Candle, Alaska, is where my story begins...

BACK TO CANDLE

Alice, dear, I wish you could see Candle and compare it with Newark.

—Sara Purkeypile, February 11, 1928

THE DECISION WAS MADE TO MOVE THE FAMILY TO Candle, Alaska, in 1925. Dad left almost immediately to start his new mining job, and Mom prepared to make the long trip alone with three young daughters. Very little could be taken on such a trip, so most possessions were left in Washington—the family would literally be "starting over" in Candle.

My mother often shared the story of her travel from Seattle to Candle. Any travel up the Alaskan coast and through the Bering Sea was hazardous. On this occasion, the conditions were windy and the seas were very rough, causing the ship to rock and pitch so violently that she feared her precious cargo might be swept overboard. To keep her daughters from falling into the frigid churning waters, Mom used a length of rope and tied Mimi, Norma, and June to her own body and then to the ship's railing.

After many difficult days on the ship, they reached Nome. They continued their journey through the Bering Strait to Deering aboard the captain's private boat. The captain was gracious enough to allow Mom to nurse Baby June in his quarters, as nursing was an extremely private matter and discretion was essential. Although the trip to Deering was delayed several hours due to icepacks that extended from Barrow to the Bering Strait, Mom and my sisters eventually arrived there safely and continued on to Candle to meet Dad. I am not sure how they traveled from Deering to Candle, but more than likely, with ice on the rivers, this portion of the journey was in a wagon pulled by reindeer.

The mining town of Candle was established on the Keewalik River at the turn of the twentieth century following gold discoveries on Alaska's Seward Peninsula. Candle grew to be the largest community on the north side of the peninsula, although the population decreased after its mining industry suffered a sharp drop in production around 1907. Mining continued as the primary source of employment, and the non-native influence was evident in the saloons, gambling houses, and houses of vice lining the main road in town.

The Candle, Alaska, post office where Audrey was born in 1927.

January 20, 1926

Dear Alice,

Candle is frozen for eight months of the year. Then, our mail comes to us by dog team. First Class and registered mail is sure to reach us, but parcel post is uncertain until the boats run. Candle is on the Kotzebue Sound away up in the Arctic Ocean— on Seward Peninsula. Take one of your children's geographies and hunt us up. Then you will realize just how far away we are and how good your letter was to us.

Mail Day is the big day in Candle, and letters are our one touch with the outside world. During the winter the mail comes every two weeks—it is usually about two months old when it reaches us. In the summer, the mail comes once a month, but it comes quicker from "the outside"—the world outside of Alaska.

Just now we are rejoicing in the return of the sun. We live by lamplight during the winter months. Now the sun is back and getting a little stronger each day—in June, we will have sunshine all the time. For about two weeks it never sets at all—we see it all the time, night and day. There really is no night during the summer months. It is a task to get the children to come in for bed.

Irus is mining here—we expect to stay three years this time—then, the girls will have to get the advantage of good schools. Irus has been coming here off and on for over twenty years—so, you can see he is an old "sourdough."

Your cousin,

Ciss (Sara)

July 20, 1926
Dear Alice,
You know in the winter it is dark most of the time, and we read a good deal. We have learned to live by lamplight in Alaska. At this time of the year it doesn't get dark, and we enjoy the long hours of sunlight. We have a nice little garden here in the Arctic. Lettuce, celery, radishes, and turnips grow well up here. There are loads of wild berries, too, which will soon be ripe.

I'm the "Hello Girl" in Candle—we live in the telephone house and have charge of this end of the service. I've just been appointed post-mistress. Both jobs put together only pay about five hundred dollars a year, but it all helps out ...

Your cousin,
Ciss

February 11, 1928
Dear Alice,
Your letter of January 6th reached me a few days ago. It came by airplane from Fairbanks to Candle—hence the speed. It usually takes from six weeks to two months over the winter trail. We do have an occasional visit from an airplane. Whenever it comes, it brings mail ... Fairbanks is seven hundred miles from here on the Chena River ... The plane flies from Candle to Fairbanks in five hours.

We are having very cold weather just now—the past two days have been forty below zero. Last week it was twenty below and blowing a hurricane for five days. Our two little girls haven't missed a day of school during the winter, but they haven't far to go and look like young teddy bears when they turn out in their furs. The reindeer is used for meat here and the reindeer skins for fur clothes, parkas, and mukluks. I don't know whether I have told you that we have to buy our supplies, groceries, coal, and clothing a year ahead. The big freight boat comes once a year from Seattle. There is one general store in Candle run by a German man, but his prices are so high that we buy everything direct from Seattle.

Alice, dear, I wish you could see Candle and compare it with Newark. Candle is just a small mining camp—gold, of course. The population of white people is about sixty, including children. In the summer, when the dredge is working, there are more men who come from the outlying districts. We have a good schoolhouse. There are ten children in school and an A-1 teacher who comes from Seattle.

We have no church or mission—the only Sunday school Candle ever had I held when I had more time. We have a movie show every Sunday night during the dark months. The films we get are ones that are sometimes ten years old, but we enjoy them because we haven't seen them. Some are very good.

There are three good radio sets in camp. Sometimes we hear stations from all over, but the Seattle ones are clearest. Japan we hear well but can't understand, of course. The elements interfere a lot. Sometimes we don't get anything for a week.

The Eskimos really do eat blubber and seal oil—it isn't just in a movie stunt. It forms a large part of their diet and seems to be necessary to keep them in health. We haven't come to blubber yet, but if we stay a few more years you can't tell what might happen. We live a good deal on canned goods—I never knew so many different things were canned until *we came to Candle. We have potatoes and onions for fresh stuff during the winter and oranges keep fairly well. Ours will keep until about March—then the next fresh supply will be here in July.*

Have I told you about Audrey Davine (pronounced Daveen) Purkeypile? Born June 15—she is a darling baby—healthy and good. We have four nice little girls. Baby is such a dear ... We are even reconciled to the fact that she is not a boy. We had ordered a Matthew David.

Your cousin,

Ciss

Summer 1928. Audrey in Candle, Alaska.

My entrance into Candle, Alaska, on June 15, 1927, in the post office living quarters caused quite a stir. Mom believed that I was the first white child ever born in the small mining town. After hearing that Irus had a new daughter, the miners came to visit the newborn sleeping in the post office in a wicker basket. Of course, one does not go calling on a new baby without bearing gifts, so I was blessed with a "baby shower." When miners come to your baby shower, you can imagine that they bring gold dust and nuggets and that's just what they brought me. Sixteen months after my birth, my mother delivered a son, Matthew David.

The four Purkeypile girls on Main Street, Candle, Alaska, 1928.

SELAWIK

Dear Alice,

I wrote you from Candle that we had made application for work under the Territorial Bureau of Education—we received appointment to Selawik. We left Candle last August. Candle is only about ninety miles from here in direct airline, but the way we had to travel—in small gas boats—it is about two hundred miles.

—Sara Purkeypile, August 10, 1929

WHEN I WAS ONE YEAR OLD, MY PARENTS WERE TOLD about a teaching opportunity in an Eskimo village by the friends who attended their wedding. After much consideration, Dad and Mom applied for the job and were accepted by the Bureau of Education of the Territory of Alaska. I recall their combined annual salary was $1,500. Years later, Mom said that the "money was good and enabled us to save for our children's education."

In August 1928, my parents loaded their young family into a small open boat and traveled the Keewalik River to Kotzebue Sound, and then proceeded by launch through the Kotzebue Sound and up the Selawik River to Selawik, Alaska. Selawik is located just above the Arctic Circle, and the village is divided by the Selawik River, with villagers living on both sides. The river is a large river, and the villagers would travel from one side to the other by boat in the summer and over the ice in the winter. (Today, the village has a bridge spanning the river to connect the two sides.) Although the tundra on both sides of the river is very flat, it begins a gradual incline north to the base of the magnificent Brooks Range.

The Purkeypile family leaving for Selawik, August 1928.

> *August 10, 1929*
> *Dear Cousin Alice,*
> *I wrote you from Candle that we had made application for work under the Territorial Bureau of Education. We received appointment to Selawik and left Candle last August. Candle is only about ninety miles from here in direct airline, but the way we had to travel—in small gas boats—it is about two hundred miles.*
>
> *We arrived here September 3rd [last year], and from then until now I have seen only one white woman. She has made two short visits here to see her son—a trader. There are two white men—both traders. There are about three hundred Eskimos.*

Selawik is one of the largest villages in this far Northern District.
Your cousin,
Ciss

Selawik had been without teachers (ug-a-lug-tees) for about four years, so when we arrived, our family was enthusiastically welcomed by the three hundred Eskimos living there. In August 1928, we began what would be a nine-year journey living among and for the Eskimo people.

My parents arrived in Selawik with the title U.S. Government Teachers. Within a short time, in addition to teaching, Dad would acquire the titles and assume the positions of postmaster, health officer, and reindeer superintendent. Mom's training as a midwife and knowledge of nutrition and hygiene would also prove valuable to the Eskimos in the village.

Our new home was the two-story schoolhouse built in 1909. It was the largest building in Selawik and sat on a small knoll in the center of the village overlooking the river. Eskimo cabins and mud igloos dotted the riverbank on either side of the schoolhouse as well as across the river.

The Purkeypiles with friends in front of
the schoolhouse in Selawik, Alaska.

Large windows lined the shingle-covered sides of the schoolhouse. The school office, classrooms, and part of our living quarters were downstairs, with two bedrooms and two large storage rooms upstairs. Lighting was provided by the Bureau in the form of gas lamps that were attached to the ceiling. Every day, Dad rose early to pump up the lamps and light the mantles. He was certain to keep many mantles in stock, as running out during the dark winters would result in inadequate lighting for the school and living quarters.

Our living quarters were in the front of the building— they included a kitchen and a combination living/dining room that was furnished by the Bureau. My three sisters and I slept in one bedroom upstairs—Mimi and Norma on a double bed and June and me on cots. From our bedroom window we looked out over the vast tundra to the Brooks Range, a mountain wilderness that stretches east and west across northern Alaska. My parents slept in the second bedroom upstairs with a view of the river and the village. When Dave was born in 1928, he slept in a bunk under the alcove in my parents' room.

The kitchen was lined with painted white cupboards that reached to the ceiling, and a round wooden table, used for food preparation, sat in the center of the room. The woodstove included an oven and warming area, and cast-iron pots and skillets hung on hooks above.

Our "plumbing" consisted of two outhouses behind the school and potty pots inside the house for nighttime use. Occasionally, the potty pots would be used during the daytime in extremely cold weather or blizzard conditions. Sometime during our nine years in Selawik, Dad installed two toilets off the schoolroom for our family's use—protecting the Purkeypile children from disease, such as tuberculosis, diphtheria, and measles, was a critical concern for my parents.

Drinking water was obtained by melting snow on the stove. A large water barrel stood in the kitchen to keep the melted snow, and a metal dipper hung on the side for dipping water. For bathing purposes, we used water from the river year round. During the winter months, the Eskimos sawed holes in the ice to access the water for bathing, as well as fishing. Most of the holes on the ice would be covered with boards to protect children from falling into the frigid water.

The Eskimos loaded water in buckets on either end of a yoke and delivered it to us on bath days. Sometimes they gave us the water for free. Other times Mom and Dad paid for the water service—Dirty Dick was one of our regular suppliers at twenty-five cents for five gallons of water. Mom heated the river water on the stove and poured it into the galvanized tin wash tub. Dad positioned the tub in front of the open door of the stove to keep us and the water warm until bath time was over. One or two at a time, we would dip in to quickly wash—Dave and I were always the last ones to bathe.

Dirty Dick delivering five gallons of water for 25 cents.

The living room was a buzz of family activity during the evening hours. A green couch provided the seating, along with two upholstered chairs. When Mom's dad came to live with us in 1934, the living area doubled as his bedroom, the green couch his bed. We called him Gramps Whitehead. Several bookshelves packed with books lined the walls of the living area. I remember children's books such as the Elsie Dinsmore series and encyclopedias and medical books. The big day was when the *National Geographic* magazine came in the mail. It was difficult for us to understand a world other than our world in Selawik, Alaska, and we would eagerly search the globe on the bookcase, looking for the countries featured in the magazine.

The long wooden plank table in the living room was the central location for eating, schoolwork, and projects. The table sat in front of a large window that overlooked the Selawik River and the Eskimo homes on the other side.

According to Mom, our ham radio was our salvation. She told her cousin, "You city folks cannot imagine what a wonderful blessing the radio is in these isolated spots. Just to hear good English is a relief from the "pidgin" English of our natives. And we get world news from two California stations every evening." From time to time, interference would prevent radio reception, and Mom would say, "I feel like we are the only people on the earth."

Dinnertime was an important gathering time for our family. Dad sat at one end of the large dining table and Mom at the other end. This was a time to talk about the day and the village news. Dad was an "on-time" person, so no one could be late to the table. He had a yardstick by his chair that was the perfect length for lightly whacking the heads of those not obeying during the meal. This is nothing to boast about, but I held the record for the most reprimands from Dad, usually for talking with my mouth full. Mom had studied nutrition in college and was committed to building up her children's immune systems. She served a variety of foods and gave us vitamins and cod liver oil daily. I know now that we would not have survived in Selawik if she had not taken such good care of us.

Very few fresh items were available in Alaska, especially in the winter. Everything was canned. Powdered milk and powdered eggs came in cans. Even cereal was in tin cans. At this point in my life, canned corn on the cob does not sound very appetizing, but in Selawik it was a rare treat. Occasionally, a government official visited my parents, and Mom always tried to serve a special dish for dinner.

On one such occasion, a man from the Department of the Interior visited the school, and my parents invited him to have dinner with us. I remember him as a big, burly fellow with big, hairy, and dirty hands. Mom, Mimi, and Norma set the bowls and plates of food on the table. When Mom brought the bowl of steaming hot buttered corn on the cob, I glanced at Dave, giving him a wink. Our mouths were already watering. After Dad gave the blessing, the food was passed and our guest began to tell us a story. I don't recall what it was about, but I remember clearly that he was in the middle of his story when our bowl of corn on the cob was passed to him. He held it for a moment and then reached in and grabbed several cobs! He stood them on end on the table as props as he continued to tell his tale. At first it was funny, and the five of us tried to contain our giggles, encouraged to do so by a stern look from Dad.

As the drama of his story unfolded, our looks to each other turned to horror. His dirty hands continued to remove the cobs of corn one by one. How many characters are in this story, we wondered? And how many of our cobs of corn will be called into service? We all kept giving Mom anxious glances. She was aware of our panic but smiled sweetly, giving us a look of warning—the look that says "Be patient, children, and don't say anything." With the bowl empty, the story finally came to a conclusion with our guest and our dad roaring and choking with laughter. When he gained his composure, the man piled the corn, *our corn,* back into the bowl and passed the dish on down the table. We were crushed. As the corn was passed, each member of our family courageously mustered a "no, thank you," and passed the corn on to the next person. Our dinner guest was the only one to eat corn on the cob that night.

Year round, the Eskimos provided us with fresh white-fish from the river. Mom's favorite recipe included baking the fish with tomatoes and onions. Duck, ptarmigan, reindeer, rabbit, and bear were all on the menu from time to time (although bear meat was black and we were not fans). Mom would make stews with some of the meats, mixing them with pasta and rice. In the summer, we gathered cranberries, blueberries, and salmonberries.

The schoolhouse and living quarters were heated with wood and coal. A large metal drum sat in the middle of the schoolroom, and our living quarters had several wood-burning cast-iron stoves that glowed with warmth through most of the year. The Eskimos made sure that the teachers had sufficient wood for the winter. My siblings and I were in charge of stacking the wood in the storage shed off the living room. Coal came in gunnysacks that were very useful for making play tents. One spring, my mother wrote to her cousin Alice, "We used twenty tons of coal and twelve cords of wood to heat the classrooms and living quarters and survive the winter cold!"

In 1931, Dad decided to dig a cellar next to the school for additional cold storage to keep food during the harsh winters. The Great Depression was engulfing people in the lower forty-eight, and Dad wanted to be sure we had sufficient food available if our supply boats failed to deliver.

> *September 14, 1931*
> *Dear Cousin Alice,*
> *You have heard of people living on an iceberg—*
> *that's us. On the 15ᵗʰ of August, when you folks*
> *were sweltering, Irus dug down about a foot and a*
> *half and hit solid ice. He was going to dig a cellar*
> *but had to stop. The schoolhouse here is built on a*
> *glacier. The glacier ground is covered with tundra*
> *and looks the same as the rest of the country until*
> *one begins to dig. That doesn't mean that we are*
> *not comfortable. We are very comfortable and glad*
> *to be where we are with such hard times "outside."*
> *Our papers and magazines are all full of the terrible times outside.*
> *Your cousin,*
> *Ciss*

Besides being thankful for our comfort in Alaska, my mother was also quite thankful for household help. In Selawik, we always had a nanny—a young Eskimo woman who cared for those of us not yet in school. She lived in a small room off the schoolhouse office. We had four nannies during the nine years we were in the village—Esther, Cora, Lela, and Minnie Kiana. These young women came to us in their upper teens and were unmarried. They were fun to be with and taught us Eskimo ways and traditions as well as some of the Eskimo language. But none of the nannies intended to work long for the Purkeypiles. Their goal was to find a husband. When one nanny married, our mom would be on the search for a replacement.

Mom also hired Eskimo women to help with laundry

every Saturday. She had a white wringer washing machine with a scrub board. On wash day, the family laundry was washed and hung on lines strung across the schoolroom; in the summertime, the damp laundry was hung outside to dry. I do remember a few instances when the items were hung outside in the cold and were frozen stiff when brought back inside.

I think Mom said it best when she said, "We are very comfortable and glad to be where we are…" She had no electricity and no plumbing. Most of the year, the weather was dangerously cold. Supplies were received once a year in July—I have always been amazed at how she carefully planned to care and provide for a family of seven one year in advance. My mother made do with very little, but always considered herself blessed.

PARKAS AND MUKLUKS

MY FAMILY WAS QUITE COMFORTABLE YEAR ROUND IN THE schoolhouse quarters. Having a living area, kitchen, and two bedrooms for eight (our family, plus Gramps) was a luxury compared to the living conditions of our playmates. The majority of the Eskimo homes were one-room log cabins with a few mud igloos scattered throughout the village. Tundra moss filled the cracks between the logs or mud blocks as well as between the wood slats on the floor of the cabins. As many as ten family members lived in one home.

Most cabins had a low wooden table in the middle of the room, standing only about six inches off the floor; the natives sat on the floor to eat their meals. Many homes did not have beds, so families slept on the floor on pallets. Selawik did not boast any plumbing; however, every family had their own outhouse. Like us, they had wood-burning iron cook stoves for heat and cooking.

Eskimo men dragging logs from the Selawik River. The logs were used for fuel in homes and in the school.

The Eskimo diet included fish, wild game, reindeer meat, berries, roots, and bread, although the bulk of their diet was dried fish dipped in seal oil or fresh raw fish. The Purkeypiles enjoyed many of the same foods, but declined the roots and raw fish. Whether dried or fresh, raw fish was never on our menu. As the Eskimo men sat around in a circle enjoying their fish, I was amazed they could do this without slicing their lips with their hunting knives. The way they ate this staple of life appeared almost ceremonial and with a kind of rhythm—dip fish into the seal oil, stick it in the mouth, then—*whack!* Chop off the excess! Over and over until the fish was gone. Meats and fish were kept in a cache, a hole dug in the ground outside the home. The Eskimos believed that this was necessary to keep the spirits of the animals and fish outside.

There was one tasty Eskimo treat that we loved to have offered to us. We would beg, "Take us, Mom! Take us, *please!*" And Mom knew exactly why we wanted to go with her to visit her friend Lucy. Lucy lived in a one-room cabin across the river from the schoolhouse. She spoke some English, so my mom, desiring conversation with other women, often went to visit her. Lucy made the best ice cream. Lucy beat seal oil and snow together with a wooden spoon until the mixture was white and creamy. After folding in some berries, the ice cream was ready to eat. One whiff of the seal oil and Mom politely declined, but my sisters, brother, and I eagerly accepted the delicious treat. In this particular case, seal oil was no problem for us!

The Eskimos were very resourceful and spent the entire year trapping, fishing, and hunting to provide for their families. They usually enjoyed great success with the muskrat hunts. The pelts from these large aquatic rodents were used as barter at the trading post. Worth one dollar each, they were traded for items such as flour, sugar, tools, and even muskrat traps to assist with the "ratting."

> *The muskrat catch was considered one of the most important of the hunting season. The entire family took part in the ratting, from the very young to the very old. One youngster, six years old, caught forty rats one year. Both gun and trap are used in the rat harvest. Some families caught as many as seven or eight hundred rats in the season.*
>
> —Irus W. Purkeypile, December 1930

Most of the parkas in the village were made from reindeer hides; year round, the women tanned the hides and prepared them for making winter coats. The parkas were meticulously pieced together, sewn with strips of reindeer sinew (tendons) and needles from the general store. Furs from other animals, like muskrat, seal, bear, rabbit, and ermine, were used to decorate the parka and long wolverine fur was typically used to trim the hoods. All of us had parkas we had received as gifts or had purchased from the Eskimos; our family called them parkeys. Dad's parkey was beautiful, made of different shades of muskrat in an intricate pattern.

Eskimo women on wood raft next to their home.

The women usually made a simpler parka for everyday wear. The fur was turned to the inside for warmth, and a calico or duck cloth dress with a hood (kusbuk) was made to cover the animal skins. In extremely cold conditions, two fur parkas were worn—one with fur next to the body, and one with fur to the outside.

Winter footwear, or mukluks, were made of animal pelts, the fur side on the inside of the sole. Heavy socks from the general store were worn for warmth. In wet weather, tundra grass was placed inside the mukluks to absorb the dampness from the ground, preventing frozen toes and possible frost-bite. The fur on the sides of the mukluks was on the outside for beauty. Beads, furs, and handwork trimmed the tops of the boots.

The summer mukluks, called oogruks, were made of tough seal or walrus hide and were waterproof. Eskimo women shaped the fronts of the oogruks, rounding out the toes with their teeth. The result was a look resembling a crimped piecrust, as well as teeth worn to the gums from the art of mukluk making. In fact, many of the women were toothless due to the stress on their teeth.

Though the natives were industrious and never sat idle, they loved to socialize with one another. The Friends Mission Church, established in Selawik around 1910, was the center of most of the social life in the village. Numerous services were held throughout the week, including three regular services and Sunday school every Sunday, prayer service on Wednesday night, Tuesday afternoon children's class, Friday young women's group, and Saturday men's group. Eskimo preachers taught the lessons in the Sunday morning services, and every man, woman, and child in the village attended all three services. Miss Honeycutt, the Friends missionary in Selawik, taught the Eskimo Sunday school with the aid of an interpreter, although she spoke fairly fluent Eskimo. Occasionally, Miss Honeycutt conducted a children's class in English for us, but most of our Bible training took place around our dining table, taught by our mother.

Our family had great respect for the Eskimo people in Selawik. Both men and women were resourceful, hard working, and committed to providing for their households. Their sense of community was strong and their rules of conduct were simple—one, all members should help each other in the struggle for life, and two, each person should live peacefully with others.

SCHOOL DAYS
IN SELAWIK

*A good education is the best thing you can give them [children].
That is what we plan for ours. They haven't much chance in this
age without a good education.*

—Sara Purkeypile

*What the Selawik people would do without the school is hard to
say. The regular school duties are only a part of the teacher's value
to the village. All the problems and troubles are brought to them
for a solution. When someone is hurt or sick, they run to the school
for help. When they need letters fixed up or mail orders added up,
the teachers help them. The teacher also directs the village council
and the reindeer company.*

—Irus and Sara Purkeypile, December 1930

THE FIRST YEAR OF TEACHING SCHOOL IN SELAWIK WAS
challenging for both Dad and Mom. Besides teaching school
all day (Dad had twenty pupils and Mom had forty), they
were managing four young children and expecting another
child. The nanny kept June and me during the day while our
mother was teaching. Mimi and Norma were in my mom's
class along with the other primary Eskimo children.

After the first year in Selawik, Mom wrote to her Cousin
Alice, "This first year has been a difficult one, as everything
is so new. My deaconess training fitted me some, but it is a

new line of work for Irus. He has taken hold and is giving good service."

All of the school children learned the value of a good education. Mom taught the primary grades, while Dad taught the intermediate grades up through sixth or seventh grade. We had some books, but many lessons were presented on the blackboard and the assignments completed on individual chalk slates. Formal education for the Eskimos ended after the intermediate grades, but my siblings and I went on with Calvert courses from the University of Maryland, home schooled by our mother.

The first school year in Selawik, 1928.

Dad loved Abraham Lincoln and George Washington and hung their portraits on the white-painted walls of his classroom. A large map of the United States was referenced during geography and history lessons.

The only wall décor I remember in Mom's primary classroom was the Bathing Chart. At the beginning of each school year, she posted a large wall chart with each student's name on it. At the end of each week, Mom said, "Okay, students. Please stand up if you took a bath this past week.

Great! Good job, Lydia. Thank you, Frank!" Standing under the Bathing Chart, Mom licked silver stars and stuck them next to the names of those who took a bath during the week. At the end of each month, a gold star was awarded to those who had earned four silver stars.

After several years, Mom decided to begin the school year without the Bathing Chart. "Regular bathing should be a habit by now!" she told Dad. A few weeks into the school year, Mom asked students to stand if they had bathed each week since school had started. Only a few children stood up. Mom was obviously disappointed. "Bertha, why have you not bathed every week?" Bertha sat next to me in class and was one of those who remained seated. Bertha crossed her arms in front of her chest, sat up straight, and boldly looked my mother in the eye. "Nothing stars, nothing bath!" The Bathing Chart went up again and stayed on the wall until we left Selawik.

Besides teaching the basics, Dad and Mom each taught extra classes after the regular school day. Mom taught sewing and cooking classes and organized an official 4-H Club. Dad taught manual training classes, instructing the boys in how to properly use tools. Word that Mr. Purkeypile had tools soon spread through the village, and the natives occasionally asked Dad to borrow something.

Sara and her 4-H Sewing Club. The young women were proud of their new parkas made from brown denim.

Missionaries taught many of the Eskimos in our village to write in English, and Dad often received notes such as the following…

> *if Government have any crying stone can I use to sharping my ax. I made it dull to used for the dig grave yesterday. if it not that be all right with me.*
>   *Your friend,*
>   *Harry*

The schoolrooms were heated with a large barrel stove that burned coal and wood. The barrel stood in the center of the schoolroom, and in the middle of winter the desks closest to the heat were very desirable property.

Wrought iron and wood desks with lids that lifted for book storage lined the wooden plank floors of the schoolroom, surrounding the heating barrel. Besides the slates, we had a supply of yellowish, course lined paper for our writing assignments, of which we had several each day.

Although the Eskimo children were not required to be in school, the sixty students attending constituted most of the school-aged children in the village. After the third or fourth grade, the numbers began to dwindle, as more children remained home to help their parents with childcare and hunting.

Mom and Dad, both called by the name for teacher, "Ug-a-lug-tee," seldom experienced discipline issues with their students. The children loved school, and they loved to please the teachers. They were also very enthusiastic about learning. Since there had been no government school for several years, the majority of the children did not speak English when we arrived in Selawik, but they learned quickly. Mom and Dad were glad when several of the Eskimo mothers who knew some English offered to take turns translating in the classroom until the children became more proficient in the language.

The Eskimo children wore parkas made of reindeer hides, and baths were taken typically once a month, if that often (even with the Bathing Chart incentive). The Eskimo diet of fish and seal oil, coupled with the parkas and bathing routine, produced an unpleasant phenomenon. The parkas soaked up the scents of seal oil and fish. When people and parkas were in an enclosed area together and the heating barrel warmed the room, the air was unbearable, especially for those not on the seal oil and fish diet. To help solve this "problem," the government school laws required that the fur parkas be hung outside the classroom in an alcove off the front office when the children came to school. With our long underwear, wool stockings, bloomers, and calico parkas (kus-buks), we were usually comfortably warm.

Whenever the weather allowed, we went outside for recess. One of the favorite Eskimo games was Jump Board, similar to a seesaw. Two students "played" at a time—one on each end of a long board that was centered over a log. One student jumped on his end of the board, tossing the other one into the air. Each tried to outdo the other with their aerial routine. I marveled at their athletic ability as they turned flips in the air before landing on their feet squarely on the end of the board.

For the less daring, we had swings attached to a tall wooden frame and balls for team games. Andy-Over was played by throwing the ball back and forth over the roof of the school. When it was too cold to be outside, even with our furs, we stayed inside and played games. Jacks and pick-up sticks were favorites, and Mom always had paper for drawing pictures.

April brought the sun, warmth, and the promise of summer to come. The closing party at the end of the school year was highly anticipated; Mom planned the party and worked for several days with her cooking class to prepare the food.

> *April 10, 1934*
> *Dear Cousin Alice,*
> *We are looking forward to the close of school again. Our closing party will be held on Friday. The cooking class does the cooking, and we give the children a big feed of beans and bread and cookies and cocoa. You would enjoy a big laugh if you could drop in while the party is in progress. The children sit in a big circle on the schoolroom floor—each one has a paper napkin for his table, a granite plate and cup, and a spoon, and we are all ready to go. Can we eat? My primaries look like a bunch of little puppies when they get through. The school party is one of the big events for the children. They look forward to it all through the school year.*
> *Your cousin,*
> *Ciss*

School was fun, but no school was even better. The end of the school year meant that my siblings and I could have Mom and Dad all to ourselves for a few months—no sharing required. While we looked forward to berry picking, picnics, and summer travel, my parents anticipated a much-needed rest from their teaching responsibilities.

SEASONS OF PLAY

We are all prepared now for another year of isolation. We are so busy we don't get much time to be lonesome. There is plenty of skating and fun with the dog sleds, so the children are happy.
—Sara Purkeypile, September 14, 1931

SOMETIMES IT SEEMED AS IF THE WINTERS IN SELAWIK lasted for years rather than months. By the end of August, the temperature dropped to freezing at night, and in September, we saw the first snow of the season. The river began to freeze and did not fully break up until the next June. Most of our winter was dark—dark and extremely cold. Occasionally, the temperature gauge read sixty or seventy degrees below zero. From November through January, the only daylight would occur between noon and two in the afternoon—and then, the light was like twilight for one to two hours.

During these dark months, the moon was our sun and the frozen river was our playground. We played for hours at a time on the ice with our Eskimo friends. All of us had Eskimo names given to us by the natives in Selawik. Dave's name was Keenuruk, Norma was Dotuk, Mimi was Menuruk, and June was Junaruk. I was Negluruk. Soon after the river froze in September, we strapped on our ice skates and skated with our friends until the first winter storm blanketed our rink with powdery snow. When Mom wanted us home, she stood on the bank by the school and blew a large silver whistle. I can still hear my playmates saying, "Negluruk, you mama wants you right away!"

Several nights each week during the winter, entire families played "football" on the frozen Selawik River, a game more like our soccer today. The Northern Lights are a spectacle not witnessed by most of the earth's inhabitants, but they were often our "stadium lights." On clear, silent nights, with the stars brilliant, the curtains of light danced and waved across the winter sky, revealing all colors of the rainbow. Sometimes they seemed to be reaching very low, almost touching the frozen river, and making audible swishing and crackling sounds. I would stand transfixed on the ice, in awe of the magnificent display of color and movement. The Eskimos said that the sounds of the lights were the people who had left this world playing games in the sky.

During the winter, large snowdrifts were created by the snowstorms—sometimes eight to ten feet deep and hard packed from the wind. My sisters, brother, and I were drawn to these drifts like magnets. We dug tunnels all through the snow and played house with our stick dolls. Inside the "house" we carved beds and ledges in the snow using the shovels from the coal buckets. Mom and Dad never seemed to worry about our playhouses caving in around us.

My parents were often amused by how much the natives in Selawik enjoyed giving us special treats, including an occasional ride on one of their sleds. Securely tucked into the sled made from animal bones, wood, and skins, the five of us were toasty warm snuggled together in our fur parkas. The musher stepped onto the back rails, gathered up the control reins, and yelled, "Muk! (Go)." Within seconds, we were flying across the frozen river. Huskies were bred long ago with wolves to instill new strength, vigor, and endurance. They loved to run and it seemed as if they went from standing still to running at top speed with one leap. "Wheee!" Our breath turned to clouds of fog around our faces as we squealed and laughed. When we became quiet, we heard the panting of the dogs and the swish of the sled on the ice in an otherwise mysterious and strange silence.

Whenever I hear the words "blizzard" or "blinding snow-storm," I always recall a certain moment in Selawik. For several days, the weather had been far too cold for outside play, so June, Dave, and I had been given permission to go next door for board games. The wood and tundra moss burning in the stove gave the cabin a definite smell of the outdoors, but we were comfortably warm and had paid no attention to the howling of the wind outside.

Engrossed in our game with our Eskimo friends, we barely heard the knock on the front door. Looking up, we saw Dad standing just inside the door of the cabin, his muskrat parka covered with snow, a long coiled rope in his fist. "Children, there is a terrible blizzard outside. Get your parkeys—I need to get you home."

"But, Dad—" I protested.

"Now, Audrey! This is a dangerous situation." Seeing that Dad meant business, the three of us scrambled to retrieve our parkas. After helping us into them, Dad tied the rope around our waists, linking us all together, him at the front of the line.

The heavy snow and strong winds kept June, Dave, and me from opening our eyes, even if we had been able to see where we were going in the winter darkness. Dad's foot-prints from his short trek to our neighbors' cabin had already been filled in and erased, so he forged new ground, pulling us behind him, until we reached the safety of the schoolhouse. If Dad had not tied us together, we would surely have been blown off the hill.

Dave and I played a great deal together, as we were so

close in age. One winter, when we were quite young and playing by ourselves, we ventured down the hill from the schoolhouse to the river. The river was frozen solid, and the Eskimos had sawed several fishing holes along the edge. A few of the holes had been left uncovered. I was a young girl of about five years old, but I do remember that one second Dave was beside me and the next he was gone. "Dave! Where are you?" Looking down through the hole, I could see the fur of his parka hood just under the surface of the water. I dove down onto the ice and plunged my hand into the freezing water, grabbing the edge of Dave's hood before he was swept under the ice. Somehow, I managed to pull him to the surface and drag him out of the hole. With our clothes rapidly freezing, we struggled up the hill to the schoolhouse. In later years, I realized that it wasn't the Lord's time for Dave to go, and He had placed me in the right place at the right time.

> *April 26, 1933*
> *Dear Cousin Alice,*
> *The children are looking forward to hours of play outdoors. Muriel (Mimi) wants to hunt muskrats. She has two guns, a small shotgun, and a .22 rifle. She is a good shot and can handle the canoe or boat as well as I can. These children of mine, because of their environment, have a different kind of play life than what we had. But they are building up strong, healthy bodies and clean minds, and that is the main thing, isn't it?*
> *Your cousin,*
> *Ciss*

Following the end of the school year, the Eskimos left the village for summer muskrat camps and fish camps. Without our Eskimo friends, the five of us played together, creating games and activities around the schoolhouse. One of our yearly activities was to build lean-tos with the gunnysacks from coal deliveries. Numerous "families" of stick dolls lived in the lean-tos in towns on the river bank, where they would often "travel" to neighboring towns to visit. The dolls were made of sticks and wore clothing made from strips of cloth from Mom's sewing basket. We spent hours scouring the tundra and the riverbanks, looking for sticks with branches for arms and legs. I recall the year that we tearfully disassembled our towns due to an impending visit from a school official. Dad wanted the schoolhouse to look "ship-shape" and thought our gunny sack towns to be an eyesore.

As all siblings experience, we had times of playing well together and times of conflict. The fact that I was a chatterbox and a busybody caused my sisters much irritation from time to time. Actually, I irritated everyone. My sister June was three years older than I am, so she was willing to play with me more than my other two sisters. Although sweet, helpful, and overall a gentle spirit, June also exhibited quite a temper when I pushed her to her limits. Her temper would be played out in one of two ways—by throwing something at me (or in my general direction) or by refusing to speak to me for days. I tried heroically to be on my best behavior and, eventually, June and I made up. She loved the stick families, and once we began playing in the tent town with our stick dolls, she forgot her anger and we were friends again.

The girls lining up in age order with their dolls on their backs like the "Eskimo" mammas, 1930.

Norma was six years older than me and was very delicate. She had experienced a series of illnesses as a young child that left her rather weak physically. The Eskimos named her Dotuk, which meant "staring." Norma was extremely shy and quiet and often hid behind Mom, peeking around Mom's skirt with her great big blue eyes. Norma loved to cook and often made Jell-O jiggles—it might seem a simple thing, but to us, this was candy! Most of her time was spent in the kitchen, helping Mom with the baking duties.

Norma loved animals. One spring Dad placed a large water barrel in the kindergarten part of the school and had it filled with dirt. Norma put mice she had caught into the barrel, and soon she had an entire mouse city. Before leaving for Kotzebue in July, Dad told Norma that she was going to have to dump the barrel of mice. Some of the men carried the barrel outside and tipped it over; new baby mice ran all over the schoolyard. Norma was completely crushed.

Regardless of the season or the game being played, Mimi—or Menuruk, as the Eskimos called her—was most often the leader. Seven years older than me, she was capable, aggressive, and took charge of any situation. We called her "The Boss." Mimi spent most of her play hours with her Eskimo friends—sledding, skating, hunting, and fishing. By the time she was fourteen, Mimi was fluent in the Eskimo language and even began dressing and acting like the Eskimos. This caused Mom and Dad concern, and they discussed the possibilities of sending Mimi to "the outside." Their desire was that we would receive a good education and eventually function well in American society, whether we lived in the lower forty-eight or Alaska. My dad made it clear, though, that he expected all of us to settle in Alaska. Alaska was home.

During the summer of 1934, Mom and Dad decided that it was time for Mimi to continue her education in the States. We were in Kotzebue for the month of July with Gramps and the nanny while our parents were in Nome attending a teacher training conference. My sisters and I were out on the tundra playing with some of the neighbor children when someone came to get Mimi, telling her to get ready to go to Nome. Mom and Dad had arranged to send Mimi to Seattle for high school, but did not tell her until she arrived in Nome. The plan was for Mimi to live with Dad's brother, John, and his family—Auntie Jennie, their three daughters, and two grandsons. They lived in a tiny house, but Auntie said that she would take Mimi for $15.00 per month for room and board.

Off Mimi went to Nome with her suitcase, traveling on a small bush plane. When Mom and Dad told Mimi that she was going to Seattle, she was crushed. Mimi moved to Alaska with the family in 1925 when she was only five years old, so her memories of a life other than in northern Alaska were very limited.

The ships were not able to dock in Nome because there

was no deep water port. Dad went with Mimi in a small rowboat out to the ship. The day was windy and the only way to get to the ship deck was to climb a rope ladder that swung wildly down the side of the ship. Mimi's adventure that day was devastating and terrifying. Mimi was so lonely and upset when she waved good-bye to Dad; she thought her parents did not love her and had totally deserted her. When Mimi climbed onto the deck of the ship, one of Mom's friends was there to meet her and see that she made the trip to Seattle safely. That night, when my sister opened her little suitcase, she found a letter that Mom had placed there. This precious letter told how much Mom and Dad loved her and how they knew she would do very well in school. Although she was upset and scared, my sister understood our parents' decision and would soon flourish in her life on "the outside."

The summer of 1934 was the beginning of change in our family, and we struggled with our loss. We had never pictured life without the five of us together. Four long years would pass before my sister returned to Alaska and I saw her again. In 1936, Norma left for "the outside" and joined Mimi in Seattle to attend high school.

OPENING ALASKA

*The airplanes are opening up Alaska and putting it on the map.
So, there is hope for even these isolated places.*
—Sara Purkeypile, August 10, 1929

AS SOON AS THE ICE WAS GONE IN THE SUMMER, GREAT
steamboats arrived along the coast with the first supplies and
mail from the "outside" since the fall freeze. The Bureau of
Education services operated the *North Star,* a ship supplying
isolated villages in Alaska.

At the beginning of each new year, Dad and Mom took
an inventory of our supplies and completed an order for the
groceries and other items we would need for an entire year.
In July, our order was delivered to Nome aboard the *North
Star,* and then the boxes and crates traveled on to Selawik
by barge. When the native children returned to the village
at the end of the summer, they ran to the schoolhouse to see
the newly delivered supplies stacked in the school rooms.
Our Christmas gifts also came at that time, and our mother
hid them immediately. I always found where she had hidden
the candy and would ask if we could have a piece now and
then. My dad ordered a box of sampler chocolates each year
as a Christmas treat. We looked forward to getting a piece;
however, we agonized over the choosing process. The name of

each piece was printed on the inside of the box, and we spent a ridiculous amount of time discussing the possibilities.

Mail order was Mom's best friend. Keeping up with clothing needs of five growing children was a challenge, and she made many dresses, pants, and bloomers from calico purchased at the general store. However, some items were ordered from a Sears catalogue, such as a pair of red rubber boots that Mom ordered especially for me.

When we first moved to Selawik, mail deliveries from the lower forty-eight were delivered to Kotzebue by airplane or ship. There, the mail was usually held until we arrived in the summer to claim it. Occasionally, a kind trapper passing through with his dog team brought the mail to us, but the territory did not have regular mail service to the villages at that time.

> *August 10, 1929*
> *Dear Cousin Alice,*
> *Your letter reached me a short time ago. It had been held up at Candle. You mailed it January 21st. Gives you some idea of how mail travels in this great Northland at times. We are ninety miles off the mail trail now, so we have to trust in some kind traveler to think of us. Our nearest P.O. is Kotzebue—ninety miles from here. However, the airplanes are opening up Alaska and putting it on the map. So, there is hope for even these isolated places.*
> *Your cousin,*
> *Ciss*

Soon after arriving in Selawik, my parents worked with the government to provide regular mail service to the village. Dad became the first postmaster in the village.

In a letter to the Department of the Interior on October 26, 1936, Dad stated his earlier commitment to this task.

> *... For two years I worked, lone handed, to secure this post office and a regular mail service. I felt it would not only be of great value for personal convenience, but also valuable in carrying on the work of the Bureau of Education.*

By the early 1930s, we received regular monthly winter mail service from Kotzebue by dog team. The children in the village ran to meet the "mailman," and my parents, welcoming an opportunity to visit with someone from outside our community, always invited him for a meal. By the early part of May, when the ground became soft, the dogs were not able to travel, and we would pick up our mail in Kotzebue in July.

The winter mail team leaving the village on the Selawik River.

> *April 26, 1933*
> *Dear Cousin Alice,*
> *Airplanes are bringing Alaska nearer to civilization all right, but I'm afraid it will be many long years before it brings Eskimo Land near enough for*

us to see that wonderful airport in Newark. I'd
rather put my faith in the auto. It won't be long
until the Alaska Highway is a fact instead of a
dream. They are building it up through Canada
clear into Fairbanks. Let me whisper this … Fair-
banks is only seven hundred miles from us over an
unbroken country. Does that make you realize how
far we are away? When we travel in this country,
we have to carry everything with us or go hungry
or "bedless."

> *Your cousin,*
> *Ciss*

Archie Ferguson, whose exploits and adventures have been documented in numerous sources, owned a trading post and general store at the north end of the village. Archie was a small man with friendly eyes, a cackling laugh, and endless energy. He traveled often between Selawik and Kotzebue, where he owned a general store and several boats. Archie's wife, Hadley, was the telegraph operator in Selawik and became a good friend to Mom.

In 1931, Archie purchased an airplane and brought air service to Selawik, an amazing advancement for our area. I often stood in front of the schoolhouse watching Archie circle his plane over the village numerous times, perhaps to check the ice or perhaps for effect, before landing on the frozen river. He operated Ferguson Airways out of Kotzebue and soon became one of Alaska's most famous bush pilots and entrepreneurs.

Like all entrepreneurs, Archie was long on big ideas. In fact, Dad said that he was one of Alaska's best "big idea guys." However, like many visionaries, Archie was sometimes short on practical implementation. My dad was the voice of reason, an implementation expert, and one of Archie's most trusted confidants. Archie often desired to share his big ideas with Dad.

These grand revelations apparently came to Archie early in the morning, because many times he came to the schoolhouse before anyone was awake. The schoolhouse door was never locked, so Archie just came on in and headed to the stairs, talking all the way. "Irus! I need to talk to you! You know that situation up in Kotzebue that we were hearing about..." Mom would hear Archie's heavy snow boots clomping up the stairs and his loud voice and would leap out of bed, scrambling for a robe. Archie was still talking nonstop as he marched up to the side of the bed to talk to Dad. I'm certain that Mom wanted to bolt the schoolhouse doors, but this never happened.

Archie was known as an ornery prankster, but was very kind to my siblings and me. I remember the day he offered us a job at his store. The five of us spent an entire day cutting down a grass field next to the store and bundling the hay. Our payment came in the form of brightly colored plastic sunglasses.

During the summer of 1936, on a trip to Kotzebue, Archie invited us to his house and showed us a Mickey Mouse cartoon in eight millimeter. We had never seen anything like this and asked to see it again and again. A few years later, Archie opened the first civilian movie house north of the Arctic Circle.

MEDICINE MEN

PUKMUK, AS THE ESKIMOS CALLED HIM, LIVED IN A DOMED mud igloo called an inni. Looking across the river from our living room window, we could see his igloo on the opposite bank. Resembling an ice igloo in shape, the house was built from tundra blocks and chunks chopped from muskeg (sphagnum moss, leaves, and decaying vegetation). Grasses grew from the top of the hut. Although I stayed a safe distance away, it appeared to be one room, based on the small size of the entire dwelling. Except for the continuous plume of smoke coming out of the hole in the roof, the hut looked more like a lodge for a beaver than a dwelling for a man. A small window was cut in the tundra blocks on one side and a heavy flap made from reindeer hides served as the only door.

Prior to our arrival, any native in Selawik who was ill or in need of medical care had only two options for treatment. One option was to travel to the nearest doctor in Kotzebue—by boat in the summer or by dog sled in the winter. This trip was a lengthy and difficult undertaking, even when one was in good health. Weather permitting, a bush pilot might occasionally be available for someone who needed immediate medical care and even surgery. The natives' other choice for medical care was to seek the services of the local medicine man, or angakok; many of the Eskimos believed that the medicine man's various potions and incantations would provide healing and "good luck."

The adults in the village kept Pukmuk well supplied with food, water, and firewood, but the Eskimo children were fearful of him—so, the Purkeypile children followed suit and claimed to be terrified of the scary little Eskimo man as well. We were not going to argue the fact, though our parents assured us that we would not be harmed.

When playing with our Eskimo friends on Pukmuk's side of the river, we gave his hut a wide berth, making a point of keeping our distance. Sometimes, we heard sounds coming from the hut or saw the flap door move as if someone was emerging and we would scatter, squealing convincingly for greater effect. "Run, Negluruk!"

The natives in our village believed the angakok to be the mediator between the natural and the supernatural world, having the power to influence events such as weather, food, and illness. He was also believed to have the ability to cure the sick and to predict future events. Many times, I watched from our living-room window as my dad crossed the river to visit Pukmuk's mud igloo. Since we were Christians, Pukmuk's religion was quite different from ours, but by reaching out to the medicine man, Dad hoped to form an alliance that would increase his effectiveness in helping the people of Selawik.

My dad entered Selawik with no medical background. In fact, he left high school during his ninth grade year, prior to taking biology or any other course related to the human body. However, soon after arriving in Selawik, the villagers began stopping by the school office to ask my dad about medical issues, seeking his help and advice. I think the Eskimos saw how wise my parents were and, because our family lived among them and treated them kindly, the natives were comfortable seeking help. I think they also understood their limited knowledge of medicine and began to think that people from the outside had the answers to their medical needs.

No doubt Dad soon realized that he needed a reliable source of medical information. He ordered a *Physician's Desk Reference* from a mail-order catalogue and, several weeks later, when the large, heavy medical book arrived with the monthly mail, our father literally vanished for hours at a time. He could be found sitting at his desk in the school office, pouring over the pages. This book was clearly off limits to the children, although I was told that I received my first spanking at age two when my dad found me tearing out a page of his valuable medical book.

Over time, and with Dad's continued successes, the Eskimos in Selawik learned to trust his medical wisdom. The schoolhouse office served as Dad's medical exam room, and the villagers came day and night to receive medical advice and treatment. I was very curious and wanted to know what was happening in the office, but was rarely allowed to be in the room when my dad was seeing a patient. Sometimes, I sat outside the door, hoping to hear the conversation, fascinated by the Eskimos' trust in the teacher's knowledge. With the *Physician's Desk Reference* open on the table, Dad set broken bones and cleaned and stitched up lacerations. Afflictions ranged from minor issues to even life-threatening accidents, such as chain saw injuries and gunshot wounds. Thankful for the medical care received, the natives often gave Dad gifts of food and furs.

On matters concerning women's health, and especially pregnancy, Mom was the medical expert and Dad's greatest resource. Not only was she a woman, but she had training and experience as a midwife. The native women in the village counted on their own midwives to deliver babies, but occasionally Mom was called on to assist.

One medical treatment that we often had to endure was Dad's favorite cure for colds and fevers. (Even armed with his medical book, Dad was still prone to concocting his own remedies for illness.) His remedy to break a fever, as well as to scare a cold away, was to give us a half cup of hot whiskey, water, and honey. I would see him coming with it and wanted to run, but knew that swallowing the horrible liquid was inevitable. We followed the doctor's orders.

As effective as Dad was as the local doctor, there were sometimes medical emergencies that were beyond his expertise. One winter, Mom became very ill and experienced terrible abdominal pain. Dad, following his medical book, correctly diagnosed her with acute appendicitis, but he did not have the means to help her. Considering the severity of Mom's pain, Dad felt the appendix was probably close to rupturing. Our friends carefully wrapped Mom in muskrat skins and lifted her onto a sled. The trip to Kotzebue was two hundred miles by dog team. Dad knew that immediate medical attention was necessary, so at his urging, Hadley Ferguson sent a telegram to her husband, Archie, who was working at his store in Kotzebue. Archie arrived a few hours later in his bush plane, and Mom was taken to the plane in the sled. Watching Mom leave the schoolhouse was a traumatic experience for all of us—we had never been apart from our mother. Dad stood looking to the sky as Archie's plane grew small in the distance and disappeared from sight; then, he returned to the schoolhouse to console his children. Mom must surely have experienced excruciating pain on the way to the hospital, but she had always been a survivor. A little over two weeks later, our mom returned home to five very happy children and a very thankful husband.

Because they lacked immunity, the Eskimos in Selawik were at risk from life-threatening diseases. Epidemics of measles, tuberculosis, and flu frequently caused many deaths, so even contact with the occasional traveler brought the potential threat of illness. Once an infection began, it could quickly spread throughout the village.

An Eskimo family. The two boys died of tuberculosis shortly after this photograph was taken.

Early one August, Dad received news of a smallpox outbreak in Deering and, shortly afterward, a traveling physician came to vaccinate the people of Selawik. Dad assisted the doctor, observing him give several vaccinations. In the absence of needles or syringes, inoculations were often given by breaking the skin and then dropping the serum into the wound. Dad knew from his study of the medical book that the recommended length and depth of the cut was one-eighth inch. He grew concerned as he observed the excessively deep, long cuts the doctor inflicted on the skin of the natives. At first, Dad was hesitant to question the doctor's knowledge, but his concern finally overpowered him and he asked the doctor about the technique. The doctor replied, "I didn't read the directions, but this is the way to do it."

In spite of my dad's reservations, they proceeded with the assault on the skin and the vaccinations.

For the next several weeks, Dad treated the natives for infections on their arms and hips from the vaccinations. Every day after school, a long line of suffering people would wait for the teacher to help them. Dad later told our family that a few of the Eskimos came very close to losing an arm due to the serious infections. He was extremely thankful that only one hundred of the three hundred villagers were in Selawik at the time of the doctor's visit, as the rest had not yet returned from fish camp. The Eskimos were thankful too. Upon their return, Dad gave them the vaccination in the proper way, according to the *Physician's Desk Reference,* and no infections developed.

As someone in the medical profession, I have always marveled at how my dad was able to piece together such a useful and accurate fund of medical knowledge. He was patient. He studied. He was also cautious and knew his limitations. Dad knew he was "practicing" his medicine on the people he cared for and who trusted him. He also knew there might not be a "backup."

In 1932, my parents received word from the Bureau of Indian Affairs that a nurse had been hired and would travel to selected northwestern villages. She was coming to Selawik! Medical help was on the way. I had never seen my parents so excited. Dad, knowing she would need a clinic and living quarters, wasted no time and enlisted the help of some of the men. They quickly built a small but very nice log cabin next to the school. The cabin was sparsely furnished but served as her living quarters and medical clinic.

The day Nurse Alma Carlson came to Selawik was a day of great celebration. For my parents, her arrival would surely give some relief to the weight of responsibility they felt for the natives in our village. Not only did Nurse Carlson provide the needed medical assistance to my dad, she was a special gift to my mother. She and Mom developed a close bond and treasured their friendship for years.

Perhaps this friendship with Nurse Carlson was born from their similar sense of calling. She was a young woman when she arrived in Alaska as a teacher and taught school in native villages for several years. Recognizing the extreme need for medical service, she returned to the States and entered a nurse's training program. Upon completing her training, she was anxious to return to serve the people of Alaska. She was assigned a vast area of northern Alaska where the only means of travel were by boat, dog team, and the occasional bush plane—not an easy task for a single woman. My parents were thankful that Nurse Carlson's schedule allowed her to be in Selawik every six months. She would usually stay for about six weeks at a time. She and Dad would set up clinic in the cabin and discuss the many medical problems in the village. Her primary responsibility was to inoculate the population against outbreaks of whooping cough, diphtheria, and smallpox. The day I understood this, I panicked. We would all have to have our shots, too! As a child, nothing seemed more terrifying than a shot. Even though the shots were inevitable, I ran and hid. But Nurse Alma had learned many things in her travels, and she knew how to lure us out of our hiding places. The next time we were scheduled for shots, Nurse Alma brought a large bag filled with beads and costume jewelry. I couldn't resist. I would do anything for a string of colorful, plastic beads—even sit bravely for my shots.

Nurse Carlson tending to the needs of the natives at a fish camp. Note the fish drying on the racks in background.

One summer, the family took Nurse Carlson by boat to visit the Eskimo fish camps scattered for miles up and down the Selawik River and adjoining waterways. Reasonably assured that I was not an intended target for her needle, I was fascinated by her work and eagerly followed her around the camps. One camp after another, Nurse Carlson relieved pain and suffering. On one of the stops, an Eskimo mother brought her daughter, a girl about my age, to the nurse. Hot with fever and crying from the pain of an abscess on her shoulder, the girl found comfort in the care of Nurse Carlson. Although Dad was always ready to move on to the next camp, we stayed there until the girl was on her way to recovery.

After returning home, I tried to imitate Nurse Carlson and sought out volunteer patients to practice my new bandaging and doctoring skills. My little brother, Dave, was usually my unwilling patient, and I became very good at setting bones that were not broken. Interesting how a single experience can shape the direction of a life. It was during this summer that I vowed to become a nurse. In an English term paper in college, I detailed my desire to enter the medical field and help "relieve the suffering of humanity."

THE WOMEN WALKED

HAVING NURSE CARLSON IN SELAWIK, EVEN IF ONLY EVERY six months, was a joy for my mom. She loved the interaction with another woman from "the outside"; politics and life in the lower forty-eight were daily topics of discussion. Through the years of working closely on the issues of Eskimo health and wellness, Mom and Nurse Carlson became fast friends, relishing opportunities to spend time together. Working as a team, they turned their attention to the Eskimo women, their personal health issues, as well as their responsibilities to their families.

With Nurse Carlson's guidance, Mom taught prenatal sessions for the native women. Teaching the women how to care for their own bodies during pregnancy, as well as how to care for their newborn babies, would hopefully result in a lower mortality rate at birth.

Each morning when I ran down the stairs to the school-house hallway, I looked to see if the "maternity box" was there. "Mom! The box is gone!"

"Millie must have had her baby last night. I will have to check on her today," Mom replied one cold winter morning. To help supply the native women with basic necessities, Mom had assembled a maternity box, complete with receiving blankets, a hot-water bottle, sterilized towels, and bandages. Day and night, villagers came to the schoolhouse to get the maternity box—the women felt they could not have a baby without Mom's special gift. When the box was missing in the morning, we knew a baby had been born during the night.

The threat of disease was constant for the Eskimos of Selawik, as well as for the Purkeypile family. To help combat the spread of germs and illness, Nurse Carlson worked with Mom to design classes for the women on personal hygiene and home cleanliness, first aid for minor injuries, and basic childcare.

One evening, Nurse Carlson and Mom sat at our dining table over hot tea and listed the expectations for the home-makers in the village. Together, they developed a list of ways the native women could keep their homes clean and talked about ways to encourage the women to comply. Each week, the women of Selawik would be asked to sweep out their cabins, wash their pots and pans, do their laundry, and wash and air out their bedding.

Every Saturday, Mom, along with a few of the leading women in the community, would walk the village, briefly visiting and inspecting each cabin. I followed along with my sisters and remember the blankets hanging out to air, women busy sweeping their cabins, and the freshly washed pots and pans stacked high. Mom carried a tablet that included the names of every family in Selawik on a chart. If the "chores" were completed and the home was in good order, a gold star would go on the chart next to the family's name. It was considered a great honor to have an entire row of stars, so the competition began! Peer pressure and a desire to please the teachers were significant factors in the success of this program. As the months and years passed, this weekly ritual became known by the Eskimos as the day "the women walked."

VIOLA

During the years in Selawik, I enjoyed the company of many Eskimo friends, but none was as dear as my friend Viola.

Viola was a sweet sister to me, although it was obvious to all who saw us together that we were in no way related to one another. I was extremely blonde and fair. Viola was much shorter than me, dark skinned, with black eyes and long black hair braided down her back.

Viola was my best friend for creative play. Dreaming as little girls do, pretending to be princesses in a beautiful kingdom, holding tea parties in the afternoon, we did everything together.

Viola and I sat next to each other in school; when it was time for recess, we ran outside together, almost in one motion, as if we were one person. Viola and I always found each other in a crowd, grabbing each other's hand and sticking together like glue until my mother called and Viola would say, "Negluruk, you mama wants you."

Although Viola and I were best friends, in many ways our lives were worlds apart. Viola lived in a one-room cabin with her large family. She was one of eight children, a fairly even mix of boys and girls. Viola slept on the floor of the cabin on a mat filled with feathers and grass (I was blessed with a cot in my house). Like all of the Eskimos in Selawik,

Viola's main diet was fish, seal oil, reindeer meat, and ptarmigan. My family ate fish, but we avoided the seal oil. From time to time, Viola and I played at her house, but a one-room cabin for ten was a very busy place. Most often, Viola came to the schoolhouse to play.

Viola's parents were George and Rosie Foster. Of course, those names, as well as the children's names, were given by the missionaries who worked in the Eskimo villages. Miss Honeycutt must have owned a large name book that she used to award "Christian" names to the three hundred natives in the village. Although Viola called me by my Eskimo name, Negluruk, I called her by her Christian name. I do not recall ever knowing Viola's Eskimo name.

During the summer of 1934, when we were about seven years old, tragedy came to our simple village. After the end of school in the spring and before the Eskimos left for fish camp, the first person became ill with tuberculosis. Each day, my parents would hear of someone else who was sick. "Doctor—please come…"

A spirit of sadness permeated the community. I could sense the fear in the adults' words to one another. Mom and Dad would speak in hushed tones, attempting to shelter us from the death we were certain to witness. My parents were very protective of us during the epidemic, and we were required to stay home most of the time, no longer allowed to run along the bank of the river to play with our Eskimo friends.

All over the village, white canvas tents were erected next to a cabin or igloo to house the sick and dying. The hope was that the fresh air would somehow help and the separation from the rest of the family might enable some to survive the epidemic. Sick family members lay on pallets on the ground under the tents. During the day, the caregivers lifted the side flaps of the tents and tied them up so the breeze could flow through and hopefully bring healing.

I recall the day that my mother motioned me to sit next to her for a few moments on the green couch. "Come sit by me, Audie." The softness in her voice told me that the words she was about to share with me would make me very sad. "Is Viola all right?" I asked. Viola was very ill and was in the white canvas tent next to her family's cabin. As a child of seven, my understanding was limited. I realized that my best friend was lying down in the white tent and could not play with me for a few days, but did not reason beyond that realization.

Within days, eight out of the ten family members in Viola's household were in the white tent. Viola's sister, Lydia, and their mother were the only ones not consumed by the illness.

When someone died, the Eskimos put a white flag on the corner of the house and the body was immediately pre-pared for burial and placed in a plain wooden coffin. The Eskimos feared that the spirit of the dead would stay in the house forever if the body was not removed quickly. In fact, the goal was to remove the loved one out of the home prior to the person's last breath so the spirit would be free and not confined in the cabin. Some would even abandon their home if a family member died inside.

Eskimo funerals were held in the Eskimo church. Every-one in the village attended, singing songs and giving lengthy eulogies. After the funeral, the natives gathered for a large potluck meal and then carried the body out to the cemetery about one half mile away on the tundra.

Prior to the influence of the missionaries, the Eski-mos buried their dead above the ground in a stick wigwam designed to keep the animals away; however, for several years the Selawik natives had buried their dead in the ground. In the winter, the permafrost prevented them from digging very deeply, so the coffin was packed with blocks of ice and piles of snow. The body stayed in this "cold storage" until the ground thawed enough to allow the men to dig the grave. This time of year, however, the graves could be dug into the ground and the body properly buried.

My family felt incredible sadness as we heard of our friends becoming ill and dying. Our mother was always attentive, but during this time her touch was especially gentle, and when she hugged us, the hold would last just a few seconds longer than usual. I sometimes caught her looking at me or my sisters or brother with tears in her eyes. At mealtime, she would say, "Eat your dinner, children. I want your bodies to be strong." And, of course, we received our daily vitamins and cod liver oil.

Dad was more quiet than usual, and I realized later how helpless he must have felt in the wake of this tragic plague. He could set a broken leg, remove a bullet from a shoulder, stitch up a wound, but he could not help the people in his village during this epidemic. I watched him from the windows as he talked to the men in front of the schoolhouse, encouraging them to have hope. Dad shook his head slowly in response to pleas for a medical miracle.

Daily, our friends came to the schoolhouse to inform the teachers of a death in their family and the schedule for the funeral and burial. Mom and our nanny were at the schoolhouse with us most of the time, but Dad was out in the village for long hours, comforting his friends and assisting with moving of the dead. Eventually, we received the news of Viola's death. She was claimed by the deadly illness, along with six of her siblings and her father, George.

The first funeral I ever attended was the one for my best friend, Viola. She was wearing the beautiful purple dress that she wore to the previous year's Christmas party. Viola's mother had made the dress from flour sacks and, with berries, she had carefully dyed the fabric a lovely dark lavender. The bodice was trimmed with lace purchased at Archie's store. Viola looked beautiful. After the funeral, the wooden box was closed tightly, and Viola was carried out of the church to make the journey to the burial ground. I stood in the school-house yard watching the long line of Eskimos solemnly following my friend in the purple dress. Never in my life had I felt a sense of loss before this day.

THE REINDEER
SUPERINTENDENT

I feel that the reindeer were given to the Eskimo, in the first place, to benefit him, and not to become a burden in later years, unnecessarily. I try not to lose sight of this as I go along with the work here.

—Irus W. Purkeypile

IT SEEMED AS IF NEW DUTIES WERE CONTINUALLY BEING added to my dad's growing list of responsibilities. Besides serving as the school superintendent, postmaster, and health officer, Dad was also asked by the Bureau of Education to help manage the reindeer herds around Selawik. Because he did not have training in animal husbandry, he did not feel very confident; however, Dad tackled this assignment, determined, for the sake of the Eskimos, to learn reindeer management and work hard to make the program succeed.

Reindeer were introduced to the natives in Selawik in the early 1900s with the delivery of two hundred forty-two reindeer from Siberia. Prior to that time, the Eskimos used the meat and furs of other wild animals, but they soon discovered that the reindeer skins were warmer and more durable. As the reindeer population multiplied, they began to replace other animals in furnishing food and clothing for the natives.

Parkas, mukluks, mittens, pants, and sleeping bags were made almost entirely of reindeer skins. The Eskimos also discovered that the meat of the reindeer was nutritious and a welcome change from the steady diet of fish. Occasionally, the hides were sold, which enabled the people to buy other necessities. More supervision and management were needed to preserve the growing herds and control the number of reindeer being harvested for food and skins.

Irus (far right) and his reindeer herders.

Irus W. Purkeypile's report to the district reindeer superintendent:

> *January 18, 1932*
> *At the request of the district reindeer superintendent, I am writing a short outline of my method of handling the reindeer business [in Selawik].*
> *Four years ago, I undertook the job of organizing and superintending my first round-up. I surely*

was some greenhorn; I didn't know a doe from a buck. Imagine how the old herders reacted to my ignorance. Though I tried not to show any more ignorance than I could help, some of it would show up once in a while. This, of course, did not tend to elevate my leadership.

I discovered that I must learn everything that the natives knew about reindeer and more, if possible. I find there are still things to be learned and improved upon.

The present system of reindeer business here has come about by a process of experiment and elimination. (It might be that we eliminated things that were good or that could be worked out elsewhere.)

I might first tell you how we handled the last yearly round-up, but in the course of this discussion, if I at times get the cart ahead of the horse, please excuse it.

The Company does not handle very much cash. It never has enough to pay wages with; so the round-up labor, if paid at all, must come out of the herd, except for regular herders or some special work, which is paid with groceries and sometimes a little cash. Regular herders, when the Company can afford to keep them, receive 30 to 40 dollars a month besides two steers or two shares.

When it was nearly time for the round-up last fall, the Board of Directors met and formulated plans for it. After they had their plans made, they called a general meeting in which everything was gone over until everybody understood what was going to happen.

In a few days, five dog teams left in as many directions, each with two men—the walker and the driver. In about one week, the first large herd arrived near the village.

Then, it was made known to all that anyone could butcher on their shares if their herding bills were paid, or if they had wages coming to them (excepting a few widow women and near destitute were allowed to kill even though no herding bill had been paid). The herd was held here nearly a week, then driven to the holding grounds. After that, no more butchering was to be done for any individual until the last day of corralling or after, and then, only for labor. The Company had butchered during the corralling more than 100 steers with which labor was to be paid. But no one was allowed to get more than a small chunk of meat until after all corralling was finished.

After the meat and carcasses were received (and some got two or three carcasses for their work), it was theirs to do with as they pleased. However, I did not allow good steer meat to be fed to the dogs if other food could be obtained, such as cull meat and fish.

All herders were not paid up at the corral, but it was understood they were allowed to butcher from the herd during the winter months until wages were paid. It was a custom for any herder or competent person with a witness to go to the herd and butcher, providing he had a permit from the local superintendent. If the local superintendent leaves, a substitute is appointed. Occasionally, the natives kill without a permit, but it [this offense] is usually reported to me as soon as possible.

Wages were paid according to this scale: dog team and driver, $7.50; walker, $5.00; herder, $5.00;

manager, chief herder, tallyman, and cook, $6.00.
The dishwashers and boys were paid $3.00 and the
skinners 75 cents per carcass. The company furnished
meals and shelter to all the workers, but not the
workers' families. Too many families at a round-up
caused a hindrance rather than a help.

We always tried to cut out not over 250 head for
a day's handling. That makes a good day's work if
it is all done well. The handling included marking,
castrating, counting, and butchering.

The reindeer holding grounds are about five miles
to the west. After passing through the corral, the
deer go out through a long lane, across a river to the
east, from which they don't get back to mix with the
holding herd.

The manager and the storekeeper at the Com-
pany Store each received $25.00 per month, paid in
groceries. When they leave for trapping, their pay
stops, but they also get extra pay for extra work.
The extra pay can be used to buy meat, skins, shares,
and pay on herding bills. The storekeeper takes care
of the equipment, buys and sells, and keeps books as
far as he is able to do so. I give him help on the books
when he needs it—and sometimes, he needs plenty.
He sells meat for $20.00 per head on foot. Whole
carcasses or front quarter bring 12½ cents a pound.
The hindquarter is worth 15 cents per pound and
the skins bring $3.00 each.

I feel that the reindeer were given to the Eskimo,
in the first place, to benefit him, and not to become a
burden in later years, unnecessarily. I try not to lose
sight of this as I go along with the work here.

Each year in November, I sum up the amount
of money and groceries that will be needed to carry

the Company through the year. This, of course, will include unpaid store bills. Then I make up the herding bills accordingly to bring that amount. Not all bills are collected, but allowance is made for that.

The margin of profit in reindeering is not great due to the lack of money among the people and the decreases of the herd caused sometimes by the wolves.

Prepared by Mr. I.W. Purkeypile
U.S. Government Teacher and
Local Reindeer Superintendent

The reindeer corrals with the herd in the distance.

The Reindeer Station and corrals were located a few miles south of Selawik on the river. Dad was very businesslike, and when I asked if I could visit the Reindeer Station, he would say, "The Reindeer Station is no place for children." But he occasionally allowed us to visit the corrals. I was proud as I watched Dad direct the reindeer round-up, wearing his beautiful muskrat parka. During the years we spent in Selawik, my dad worked with the natives in building the herds up to as many as twenty thousand reindeer.

The government realized that very few people outside

of Lapland had extensive experience with reindeer management (Lapland is a region spanning four nations: Norway,
Sweden, Finland, and Russia. The southern border is com-
monly accepted as the Arctic Circle). They imported not
only reindeer herds, but Laplander herdsmen to support
the program. Our Laplander was Johnny Ronno. He came
to us during the spring, arriving with the reindeer that he
and others had herded across Siberia and then loaded on a
ship to cross the Bering Sea. He eventually charmed us with
his chronic toothy smile, but the first time we met him, he
seemed most peculiar to us, as if from another planet. One
evening, Dad brought Mr. Ronno home for dinner. When
our guest walked into the living quarters of the schoolhouse,
my sisters and I tried to not laugh out loud. The first thing
we noticed about Mr. Ronno was his funny hat. Made of
wool, it had two horns that stuck straight up, making him
resemble a court jester. His socks were peculiar, too—red
and white stripes and pulled over his pants up to his knees.
His outfit was completed by unusual reindeer-skin shoes
with pointed toes that turned straight up at the ends. His
wrinkled brown face and hands had the look of well-worn
leather, hardened from exposure to the cold weather, like the
Eskimos in Selawik.

Although Mr. Ronno spoke virtually no English, he
and Dad managed to communicate about every aspect of
reindeer husbandry. Through a combination of descriptive
sounds and animated hand motions, they "discussed" how
to feed the reindeer, herd them, and butcher those selected.
Over the next several days, we witnessed a number of these
discussions at the dinner table through pantomime. Mr.
Ronno was a kind man and a patient teacher. Fortunately,
Dad quickly grasped the butchering process and we were
spared a repeat performance on this topic.

Irus (in his muskrat parka) overseeing the reindeer butchering.

The challenge of building up a herd when facing lethal elements, an abundance of predators, and disease must have been great. In a letter to C.L. Andrews, U.S. Government Official, on April 4, 1936, Dad wrote:

> *Last summer there should have been 14,000 Selawik deer on the range. But owing to the later rains last fall and freezing up quickly, several inches of ice covered the range. This lack of feeding ground, together with the menace of wolves, caused a great loss. More than 9,000 deer starved or were killed by wolves.*

In a letter to the U.S. Department of the Interior, Dad expressed his concern about another serious threat to the reindeer program. The program was intended for the Eskimo, but like most enterprises, men, desiring to become wealthy, sought to gain control of the reindeer herds for their own advantage. Dad recognized that these men did not care about the welfare of the natives, nor did they share the original vision and intent of the reindeer project. If the government did not intervene, the large corporations might put everyone else out of business.

C. L. Andrews shared Dad's concerns. In a letter to Dad, Mr. Andrews stated the following:

> *This matter is bigger than party or politics. It means that the comfort and destiny for future years of nearly 20,000 people [is at risk] ... The Eskimos are nearly one-third of Alaska's population. No one else can and will take care of the deer in that bleak country.*

Dad felt his first responsibility was to the Eskimo natives and their survival. *I try not to lose sight of this as I go along with the work here.*

GIFTS OF LOVE

THROUGH THE YEARS, I HAVE BEEN ASKED FROM TIME TO time to give a talk about my life in Alaska. When I was planning for a particular commitment, I decided to ask my mother to write down her thoughts about Christmas in Selawik. I could see from her letter that this was a special memory for her as well.

> *Dear Audrey,*
>
> *As the Christmas season draws near, our thoughts turn to Christmas days of by-gone years. I think that one of the most memorable ones ever was a Christmas spent among the Eskimos in Selawik, Alaska, when you were a small girl.*
>
> *The Eskimos are a happy, fun-loving people, and their happiest and most joyous time of the year is during the Christmas week. Of our three hundred and fifty people, not one would be absent from the village at that time. Some of them came by dog team from trapping camps as far away as one hundred and fifty miles.*
>
> *On this particular Christmas, the school children had worked hard for weeks on a special program of recitations and songs. The children love to take part in a program, and the Eskimo parents, like par-*

ents the world over, love to watch and listen to their own children [perform]. This year, the children did exceptionally well. There was a huge Christmas tree; also, Santa Claus was there with goodies and small gifts for all.

We had a visitor that year—a young count from Sweden. He was a musician, and after the children's program, he sat down at our old school organ and held the people enthralled for an hour with his music.

The school (ug-a-lug-vik) holds Open House throughout the week. One night is the annual party or banquet, where the guests all sit on the floor with the food on paper napkins in front of them. Other nights, there are games, music, and feats of strength. Out-of-doors there are races—foot races, dog-sled races, and snowshoe races. All very interesting with plenty of fun.

To me, the big night was the one when we all met at church. The Eskimos had prepared this party themselves. There was no tree, but they had strung up wire lines across the church on which to hang the unwrapped gifts, mukluks, skins, bundles of dried fish, bundles of fresh fish, cans of seal oil, boxes of frozen berries, parkeys, birch baskets, spoons, and dishes carved from wood—all work of the peoples' hands. The tags were made of cardboard tied on with string, but to me they seemed as beautiful and full of meaning as our most beautiful Christmas tags.

After an evening of singing carols and reading the beautiful Christmas story in English (interpreted into Eskimo for the benefit of the old folks), the Elders of the church passed out the gifts with much hilarity and fun.

Unlike our people, all gatherings of the Eskimos are held in the school or church. There are no home parties—due to the fact that the people live in one-room cabins built of logs or in one-room igloos.

After New Year's Day, the people are ready to return to normal living and duties—until next Christmas. Christmas time has followed the same pattern in Selawik ever since the church and school have been there. Simple things delight a simple people.

I hope you have enjoyed reading this, as I have enjoyed writing it.

With love,

Mother

In Selawik, I enjoyed every child's dream—three Christmases! One at the school, one at the Eskimo church, and our family celebration at home.

The Christmas celebration at the school was the highlight of the school year. For weeks we practiced reciting poems or short stories having to do with Christmas. All of the school children took their turn standing up in front of the assembly and delivering their memorized "pieces" while the parents sat cross-legged on the schoolroom floor, all with big smiles. After completing his performance, one of my classmates said that all he could see was a sea of teeth. The Eskimos were normally a happy-go-lucky bunch, but we observed that they had more fun at Christmas than at any other time of the year.

Our village Christmas tree was a beautiful spruce, which had been carefully handpicked at the timberline and strapped to a dogsled for the journey to the schoolhouse. Every year, Dad had to remove a window from the school to get the tree inside, and when it was righted, the tip hit the ceiling. The tree was decorated with brightly colored birds that had been purchased by previous schoolteachers. Numerous handmade gifts for our family, including mukluks, parkas, and toys, were placed under the tree by our Eskimo friends. I still have one of the toys, a noisemaker made from the intestine of a reindeer. It had a mouthpiece at one end that enabled me to blow it out straight like the typical New Year's Eve party blowers.

The young girls had their own reason for anticipating the Christmas party. Following the yearly tradition, all mothers in the village made a new dress for each of their daughters, the details of which would be kept secret until the party at the schoolhouse. My mother entered into this tradition as well. Most of the Eskimo women were accomplished in their sewing abilities. Typically designing their creation from flour sack material, the women dyed the muslin fabric to lovely shades of lilac and orange with berries and tree bark. Our dresses were made from calico purchased from Archie Ferguson at the local trading store.

The next evening, our family attended the Eskimo Christmas celebration at the Friends Church. The church had been built several years earlier by missionaries and was in the center of the village. This party was very lengthy, mostly due to the fact that the Eskimos loved to sing and sang every Christmas carol in the book that night. The hymnal *The Best of All* was called the "Besta Ball" by the Eskimos. Even though their singing was monotone (one could barely distinguish one note from another) and without the help of instruments, they sang with great enthusiasm and joy.

Because the Eskimo cabins were too small for parties, the natives exchanged their Christmas gifts to each other at the church. Hundreds of unwrapped gifts hung from wires strung across the ceiling. The room was wall-to-wall Eskimos and the children pushed their way around the room standing on their toes, attempting to find their name on a cardboard tag dangling from a gift. My mom called them "gifts of love." The elders removed the presents from the wire one at a time, calling the name of the intended recipient. When the person was identified in the room, the elder threw the gift across the room and to the recipient, right over the heads of everyone in between. Bundles of dried fish, fresh fish, furs, buckets of berries…whatever the gift, it was thrown to the receiver partly to add to the hilarity of the evening and partly because one could not move freely from one side of the room to the other. Since everyone received at least one gift, the party lasted for hours. During the next few days, the Christmas festivities continued with games, competitions, and "feats of strength." Many of the Eskimos' relatives came from other villages to Selawik and were openly welcomed by the villagers; the sense of family, friendship, and community was never stronger than at this time of year.

Long before Christmas, we began our search for the five largest black stockings available in the Purkeypile living quarters. No holes would do. On Christmas Eve, each of us placed our stocking at the foot of our bed before going to sleep. By morning, the stockings would be filled with nuts, hard candy, and small items, such as hair ribbons. Each stocking had one other item—a personal favorite food item. My favorite food was peanut butter, so every year I found a jar of peanut butter stuffed down into the black wool stocking. Now, bacon grease was not high on my list, but my sister, Mimi, loved to spread it on hot toast. A large jar of bacon grease, carefully filled and sealed, appeared in Mimi's stocking year after year. Norma always received a box or two of Jell-O, June had a jar of honey, and Dave's stocking usually held a bottle of catsup.

For some reason, the four girls always lined up in order of age, whether we were posing for a picture or sitting on the bed early on Christmas morning. I was always in the fourth position. Year after year, we could be found sitting on the double bed in chronological order—Mimi, Norma, June, and me—dumping out the contents of our Christmas stockings. All of the candy was pulled into a pile and the selection process began. Since I was the last in line, I always ended up with the candy no one else wanted—the licorice.

We delighted in simple things.

WHEN THE WATER RUNS

We live with and for the Eskimo all winter, but our summers are our own.

—Sara Purkeypile

OUR SUMMERS WERE DEVOTED TO FAMILY. WHEN THE school year came to a close in mid-April, the celebration began by winding up the Victrola and spinning the record "Happy Days Are Here Again." Dad loved to dance and was very good, given the many masquerades he attended as a young man in Seattle. Each of us clamored for a turn to dance with Dad on the wooden plank floor that had magically become our ballroom. Swirling and twirling in circles around the Victrola became the Purkeypile ritual to initiate and welcome spring.

Mom rarely complained about anything, but after enduring the long winter months, she would say that she was a bit tired of the "big expanse of whiteness on all sides." Though the winters in Selawik were very cold and dark, by the end of April, we began to "see the light." The temperature continued to drop to zero at night, but the days were warming up. Every day blessed us with seven or eight more minutes of daylight than the previous day.

In the spring, patches of green ground began to appear, and bright magenta fireweed and tiny blue forget-me-nots poked through the multi-colored lichen carpet. Many types of birds visited Selawik, even canaries and other types of birds that had wintered as far away as South America, Africa, and the Antarctic. The universal herald of spring, the robin, also came to our world in northern Alaska—the first birds to appear before the snow even melted. Every spring, my sisters and brother and I held a contest to see who could spot the first robin of the season.

Salmonberries began to appear in May, and they covered the tundra like a colorful blanket. Slender stems held a bright pink flower revealing a salmon red berry, resembling a blackberry in all but color. Not only were the salmonberries a tasty treat and fruit source, but the Eskimo women used them to transform white flour sacks into lovely red dresses. The berries, when crushed and strained, yielded a deep and beautiful crimson dye.

Occasionally, we enjoyed salmonberries with our daily tea. My mother, having English roots, took time every day to sit with a cup of hot tea. "Without any pros or cons, we will take time for tea," she would say. My sisters and I sat around our mother, sipping our tea and begging her to "read" the tea leaves. She would look into the bottom of the cup thoughtfully. "Well, my tea leaves say that Audrey is going to be a very good girl today." Sometimes she said, "My tea leaves say that we will have a very special treat for dinner tonight." The four of us would giggle and look at the tea leaves, wondering how our mother could read the leaves so well, and hoping that she would pass this skill on to us one day.

The frozen river was still our highway in April and early May, but by June 1, the ice was beginning to break apart. The sounds were unmistakable. Sometimes large chunks of ice broke apart violently; crashing sounds could be heard for miles reverberating across the frozen tundra. Occasionally, when lying in bed late at night, I heard the river groaning and moaning, as if a great monster was awakening. Each morning, my sisters and brother ran with me to the bank to mark the water's progress. We knew the danger, so we kept our distance as we watched the giant chunks of ice race by.

These signs, indicative of the approaching summer fun for us, meant possible danger for others. Dogsledders who traveled the frozen highway all winter were sure to listen carefully in May and June for the sounds that could mean disaster for them and their dog teams. Finally, by the first week of July, the ice was gone and the boats could run freely. We had arrived—this was the eagerly anticipated time of year that Mom referred to as "when the water runs."

In April, at the close of each school year, the Eskimos prepared to leave Selawik for muskrat and fish camps. This was their time of harvest, gathering the provisions they would need for the rest of the year. Since the river was still frozen when they left, the Eskimo families traveled out by sled and dog team. Women, young children, and babies were packed into the sleds with the supplies while the men took their post on the back or ran alongside. We watched this grand exodus from the bank of the river, waving good-bye to our friends until the last family pulled away from the village.

Every spring, like salmon revisiting the stream where they were born, Eskimo families returned to the same camps where their fathers and grandfathers had found good hunting and fishing before them. Some families traveled to Kotzebue, set up white tents on the sand, and hunted for whale, walrus, and seal. Others drove their teams inland on the Selawik River as far as the foothills of the Brooks Range, where they camped on the banks of the river and fished for whitefish and salmon.

While the villagers were away, our family made grand plans for our summer. During this time, my parents caught up on school reports, home repairs, and sewing projects. Several years ago, I read some of Dad's education and reindeer reports sent to the Department of the Interior. As I read them, I realized how thorough he was and how seriously he viewed his responsibilities. We busied ourselves with out-door games, fishing, and picking berries.

After completing his government reports, Dad some-times slipped away for one or two weeks in May. I recall waking up one morning to find that Dad had packed his panning equipment; he went to meet with some prospectors and check on some of his earlier claims. It seemed as if Dad was driven by a mysterious desire—perhaps it was the same desire that brought him to Alaska as a young man. I don't think this yearning ever left him, and I did not understand. Although Mom tried to explain it to us, I doubt that she fully understood the passion that drove Dad to search for gold.

The family on the Keenuruk.

July always meant an adventure on the *Keenuruk*. With the help of some Eskimo friends, Dad built the six-foot wide, twenty-foot-long boat soon after arriving in Selawik.

It must have looked like we were sailing into battle with a large American flag standing tall on the front deck. We called the flat-bottom wooden boat a houseboat—and the boat did have a cabin. In fact, the cabin was almost the width of the boat and ran most of the length, short four feet in front for a deck. I remember that my dad, fully six foot tall, could barely stand up straight inside the cabin. Bunks hung on both sides for the children, the nanny, and Gramps. Mom and Dad's bed lowered down from the wall, resting over the inboard engine at the back of the boat. Like the captain of his navy, Dad stood at the back of the boat, manning the steering wheel, expertly maneuvering the rivers and creeks.

Every summer in July, we loaded the boat with provisions and traveled the waterways, usually heading to Kotzebue so Dad and Mom could attend district teachers' meetings. Leaving Selawik as soon as the water ran freely meant leisure travel with stops along the way to picnic, camp, and swim. As Dad steered the *Keenuruk* downriver, I stood on top of boxes inside the cabin, peering out of the small windows and waving to the Eskimos camping on the gravel banks.

On these family trips, each child had a special job to do when we anchored on the shore. Prior to beaching, we all identified our job. Norma was always the one to find the "bathroom"—a limb hanging conveniently close to the ground. June looked for fresh water, and I was in charge of picking up sticks for the fire. Dave was very young, so he usually just played, and Mimi was the self-proclaimed "boss" in charge of the rest of us.

One of our favorite camping spots on the way to Kotzebue was on a long spit—a gravel bar protruding out into the Selawik Lake. Though seemingly lifeless and barren, this small piece of Alaska became our adventure land. After months of snow and ice and freezing temperatures, exploring the shoreline and gathering "treasures" into piles on the sand and gravel was a child's dream play. Although the river was covered with ice only weeks earlier, we swam at every opportunity. Dad and Dave jumped into the frigid water in their long johns, and Mimi, Norma, June, and I swam in our summer parkas. Mom stayed on the shore cooking on the camp stove over an open fire, laughing at the squealing sounds coming from the water. When all lips were blue and teeth were chattering uncontrollably, Mom came to the water with towels and blankets, wrapping each one of us tightly and leading us to the fire. Since I had no concept of "the outside," I thought everyone experienced adventures like this!

Swimming in the Selawik River, July 1933. The river was covered with ice just a few weeks before this photo was taken.

A small rental house on the Kotzebue town square near the hospital and school became our temporary home for the month of July. Our nanny and Gramps were with us during the day, freeing Mom and Dad to attend the teachers' meetings. My mother described the other teachers as "a jolly crowd." After a year in Selawik, my parents were more than ready for fellowship and conversation with teachers from other school districts. Mom and Dad often remarked that they had much to learn about teaching, and Mom would say, "So many needs, so much to learn."

Kotzebue was the nearest port on the Arctic Ocean. The *North Star*, the supply boat for the schools managed by the Bureau of Education, docked in July, and hundreds of boxes of supplies were unloaded. Furniture, school supplies, tools, clothing, shoes, canned goods, fresh foods, and the ultimate treat—eggs. These "boat eggs," as we called them, were carefully transported home at the end of July. When we arrived in Selawik, the eggs were taken immediately to the cellar under the wood shed. For the next few months, Mimi and Norma were in charge of turning the eggs every week to help keep them fresh, although they rarely lasted until Christmas.

"Ayeee! Kilalugak! Kilalugak!" The commotion on the beach caused us to look over just in time to see the Eskimo hunters hauling two large white beluga whales up on the sand. Several six-man teams in skin-covered kayaks called umiaks had located the whales, killed them with harpoons, and towed them back to shore. Standing on the long wooden dock where we had been fishing for flounder, we could see dozens of natives running from all sides to see the whales. These two belugas would provide enough meat and blubber to feed several families for months. I called to my sisters and brother, pointing to the men lifting their tools high above their heads. We held our breath as the Eskimos began cutting into the whales, carving out large chunks of blubber with long-handled spades, knives, and axes. The men passed the chunks of raw blubber around the circle, savoring each bite. Within minutes, children were all around the fisherman, begging for a piece of flipper, one of their favorite foods. "Talibuq! Talibuq!" they pleaded repeatedly until one of the fishermen cut some chunks of flipper for them to eat. *Yuck*, I thought. We simply stood and watched, but perhaps the next generation of Purkeypiles would clamor for the treat one day.

After the excitement subsided, the native hunters delivered buckets of blubber to their wives, who pickled the chunks with vinegar and stored them in coffee cans. The Eskimos used almost every part of the whale—the heart, the muktuk (skin and blubber), the meat, as well as the major organs. Baleen was used for weaving baskets and artwork. Masks were made from the whalebone. Women used dried sealskin to make long pouches, or pokes, to hold whale oil. Year round, whale oil and seal oil were used as a dip for softening dried fish.

Large wooden racks could be seen up and down the beach, each loaded with large strips of whale meat hanging to dry. The whale's tail was left to ferment all summer and was eaten when the ice began to form on the water. The frigid natural environment was perfect for refrigeration; muktuk and other whale foods buried in snow-covered pits in Selawik provided sustenance when hunting luck dried up and fresh meat was unavailable during the winter.

Dad spoke often of the effects of commercial whalers in the Bering Sea. During the second half of the nineteenth century, whalers from other parts of the world had discovered the resources of the Alaska coasts, greatly reducing the numbers of whales available for the Eskimo hunters in the 1900s. This was why each whale catch by the Eskimo sustenance hunters was cause for jubilant celebration.

———

My dad lived for these few precious weeks in the summer when his duties as U.S. Government teacher, village physician, and reindeer superintendent were placed on hold until the Eskimos returned to the village. His passion for gold mining was deep, and he and the other prospectors always held out hope for finding a vein of gold. Occasionally, we did not go to Kotzebue, but instead went inland, up one of the rivers to the foothills of the Brooks Range. The mountains that had represented only a distant and majestic backdrop across the tundra from Selawik now became our grand summer playground. Here, at the base of the mountains, Dad panned for gold in the adjoining creeks, hoping to find a strain—the mother lode. Camping on the riverbank for several weeks, we spent our days picking berries and playing in the woods. I remember seeing moose and caribou, but we were careful not to stray far from camp because there were also bears in the area. Although my parents were very protective of those family times, we sometimes stopped to visit our Selawik friends in fish camps on the way to the foothills. One of my first observations upon entering the camps were the millions of flies crawling on everything. The only way to preserve the freshly caught fish was to dry it, so raw fish hung all over the camps on racks made from wooden rods. The less-desirable parts of the dried fish were stored to feed the sled dogs in the winter. This was no problem for the sled dogs. They were always ravenous and quickly gulped down anything their owners fed them.

Camping in the foothills of the Brooks Range.

The natives did not seem to notice the flies swarming on the drying fish and in and around the white tents. When the fish were sufficiently dry, the women untied them from the racks and wrapped them into bundles with wire. While the men were fishing or hunting for muskrat, bear, and caribou, the women dug for edible roots or picked berries. This was the time for storing up for the winter months, and no one sat idle. As women watched their young children play, they tanned hides, sewed, or made mukluks in preparation for the approaching winter months ahead.

When Dad gathered his pans, loaded the family and food on the *Keenuruk,* and headed up the Kobuk River, we knew he had the gold itch. One time, we took our favorite dog, Rollo, for a day trip. Rollo loved us and always protected us; we were sure he was a German shepherd, a noble police dog. Jet black, his ears flopped over and his tail curled up high over his back. (Years later, when inspecting a picture of Rollo, I was disappointed to discover that he looked more like a mutt than a police dog.) Rollo was our constant companion in Selawik.

Panning opportunities were endless in the numerous creeks running off the river. Dad stopped the boat often and panned the creek while Mom cooked and we played on the banks of the river and swam. Rollo exercised his freedom, running off into the woods, but circling back to camp to check in periodically.

"Time to go! Everyone load up!" Dad called at the end of the day. The five of us were on the river bank playing, but where was Rollo? We called and called his name, but Rollo did not come. When Dad said we had to get back, the begging began. "Dad, please! We can't leave without Rollo!" We did leave, but our dad ended up with a boatload of crying children all the way home. Upset about leaving without Rollo, we begged and begged Dad to go back for him. A couple of days later, Dad could no longer take the long faces and puffy, red eyes—he left by himself to search for our dog. When Dad arrived at the picnic spot, there was Rollo, lying on the bank of the river, exactly where the boat had been beached. "Well, I'll be, Rollo. Looks like you met your match." Rollo's entire face was covered with long, yellow, porcupine quills, indicating a distressing encounter. When Dad brought Rollo home and led him into the schoolroom, he used a pair of pliers to gently pull the quills out one by one. All of us were crying, but Rollo sat still like a soldier at attention and did not make a whimper. After the last quill was pulled from Rollo's face, Rollo licked Dad's hands in gratitude.

Dad leaving on a prospecting trip with his assistant, Rollo.

Alaska is a land where migrations of waterfowl and caribou herds mark the change of seasons. Just as the dramatic exodus of the Eskimo families from the village to their fish camps heralded the beginning of our summer, their return to the village meant summer was coming to a close and winter was approaching. Eskimo families stayed in their camps until late July, storing up fish and game for the winter. Before they could return home, each family constructed a large log raft and loaded children, dogs, sleds, and tents on the floating platform vessel. Bundles of dried fish, game, and berries were packed into coffee cans and galvanized buckets for the winter months. These floating armadas slowly drifted downriver to Selawik. Those who went to Kotzebue had to return upriver to Selawik. Our friends waved and called to us from their rafts as we jumped up and down on the bank, waving wildly and calling back. The ritual lasted for several days as, one by one, the families returned to their cabins. Every item the Eskimos brought back was used, including the logs from the rafts. For two or three weeks, the village bustled with activity as the Eskimos chopped wood, repaired and built homes, stored food, and prepared their cabins for winter.

The return of the Eskimos signaled the end of our few short weeks of swimming, boating, and traveling—summer was over. In early September, my parents again opened the schoolhouse. The dropping temperatures, falling snow, and freezing river pointed toward the coming of many months of winter. Regardless of the season, I loved Selawik. I was always disappointed when summer came to an end, but could also look forward to our many winter activities. Although my mother was always positive and content, she mentally prepared herself for another winter.

SUMMER ON
THE YUKON

October 26, 1936

Dear Cousin Alice,

Our Alaska chief paid us a visit this past summer and has granted us a one-year educational leave. So we are planning on going to Seattle sometime in May. Take the whole family and stay outside a year. That will give the three younger children a term in the city schools. We will live in Seattle. All the family is counting the days now—we are so excited over going out to the girls. It is twelve years since we have been out.

I suppose all the excitement back your way is the presidential election. Who do you want to see go in? We hear the speeches over the radio, but we have no vote in Alaska. Landon sounds like a good man, but I'm wondering if it would be as well to let Roosevelt in on some of the plans. Of course, we can't get the same viewpoint as you folks on the outside, especially you eastern people.

Your cousin,

Ciss

DURING THE SUMMER OF 1936, MY PARENTS WERE GRANTED a one-year leave from their teaching duties in Selawik. A full year to live in Seattle with all of the family together again! We had not seen Mimi for over two years, and Norma had "gone out" to Seattle the previous summer. One year to read a daily newspaper and know what was happening in the world, one year to travel to visit relatives, and the chance for my mother to meet her dear cousin Alice for the first time.

Several months before the leave of absence was to begin, Dad heard from a traveling miner about a roadhouse and general store for sale in Poorman. This small gold-mining camp was in the Alaska interior, about three hundred fifty miles southeast of Selawik. Dad must have had it in his mind for some time to purchase the Roadhouse before he told us, as we did not find out until right before we moved. I have often wondered why Dad made this decision, especially in light of his wife's joy over the upcoming leave in Seattle. By this time, Dad's experience and training equipped him to make a living in Alaska, and perhaps he was less certain about his prospects on the outside. His heart for mining, the lure of being a respected storeowner, or a desire for change may have been factors in his decision. I am sure there were many discussions in my parents' bedroom at night regarding this move, some, no doubt, with passion and emotion, but my parents kept these matters private. I was only aware of the outcome as the plans for the move started into motion.

My parents told us about Poorman just a few days before we left Selawik. Since Dad did not know the condition of the Roadhouse, he planned for us to live in Ruby for the summer while he prepared the living quarters for the family. Mimi and Norma were in Seattle, but June, Dave, and I were devastated. What kind of life would be waiting for us in a mining camp named "Poorman"? I had lived in Selawik for nine of my ten years, so this life among the Eskimos was all that I had known. Selawik was home. The thought of leaving our friends and our way of life was almost unbearable. This must have been the reason Dad waited until the end to tell us. Shortening the amount of time spent grieving was probably the best plan for us, as well as for him. The most regrettable situation, however, was that Dad told us after most of the Eskimos had already left for summer camps. We were not able to say good-bye to our friends. Perhaps this was hard for Mom and Dad as well, and they wanted to spare themselves this difficult task.

The Eskimos in Selawik had grown to love and depend upon my parents and greatly respected them. Whenever the villagers had need, my parents were there to help. Akawin, the head of the Eskimo council in Selawik, was still in the village when Dad announced our plans to move to Poorman. When Akawin came to visit us at the schoolhouse, his voice was heavy with emotion, and he spoke slowly. "Many, many go mucky-muck hill (to the cemetery) when you ug-u-lug-tees (teachers) leave us." I knew the people of Selawik would be heartbroken when they returned from camps in August to find us gone.

We left Selawik in June of 1938 and traveled to Ruby, a mining and port town on the Yukon River, sixty miles north of Poorman. Archie Ferguson flew us in his airplane, taking off from the river on pontoons. Dad and I were the first to leave the village. As we walked away from the schoolhouse to meet Archie, Mom was standing in the pantry off the kitchen, scrubbing the shelves, for she desired to leave the living quarters cleaner than she had found them. That was her way.

Archie flew Dad and me directly to Ruby, so we bypassed the big city of Fairbanks, which I didn't see until several years later. I do not know why Dad chose me to fly first to Ruby, other than the fact that we flew on my tenth birth-

day. So, off we went on June 15, 1937. As I felt the new
and strange sensation of lifting up and being suspended in
the air, I was transfixed by the scenes that zoomed below
the airplane's pontoons. I was looking down on the tops of
the Eskimo cabins, and water was everywhere. I could see
our river stretch far into the distance and, as I flew higher,
I thought I could see it enter the ocean. The view from the
air was magnificent, and my face ached from being pressed
against the window as I strained to see my country from
this new vantage point. Since there was not an airport in
Ruby, we landed on the Yukon River—my first airplane ride
and we took off and landed on water! Archie switched the
engine off and the plane coasted smoothly to the shore. (I
didn't know if Archie was a skilled pilot or not. Perhaps the
fact that he flew so many years and was still flying was proof
that he was, but that day, everything he did seemed perfect.)
We deplaned by climbing out onto the pontoons and jump-
ing to the bank of the river. Archie made two more trips
from Selawik to Ruby, delivering Mom, Gramps, June, and
Dave. I am not sure what we did about our belongings, but
when our parents moved from place to place, they usually
left everything behind but the bare essentials and the pickle
fork and olive spoon.

Before the other family members arrived, Dad and I
spent a day alone in Ruby. We made our way to the general store on the waterfront for some supplies and to inquire
about a place to stay for the summer. While Dad purchased
the supplies, I stood in front of the long counter, peering
into the glass case at a beautiful doll in a wedding dress.
My longing did not go unnoticed. Dad bought her for my
birthday, as well as a pair of overalls. I must have been quite
a sight, walking around that mining town in my "Big 'n Tuff"
overalls, fresh out of the Eskimo village, carrying a doll in a
wedding dress.

Built on the Yukon River, Ruby was a collection of crudely built houses and buildings lining the muddy, rutted streets. As in most of the mining towns, the inhabitants were mostly single white men, but we were glad to see there were some families with children as well. In Ruby, the familiar faces of the Eskimo were replaced with Indians. Dad used to say that around every bend of the Yukon River was a different dialect, referring to the large number of Indian tribes in Alaska. I do not recall seeing an Eskimo during the time we were there.

The sawmill at Ruby with the Nenana in
the background on the Yukon River.

A large saw mill provided employment for most of the men in the town between gold strikes. The main road into Ruby from the boat docks was lined with saloons and restaurants and there was even a hospital. Since Ruby was a "port city," it bustled with travelers coming and going on the large paddlewheel boats docking almost daily. The *Nenana,* the largest and one of the more popular boats, came to Ruby every couple of weeks, bringing mail and supplies. Along with most of the townspeople, we ran to the banks of the Yukon to watch the *Nenana* coming down the river.

Dad rented a two-story clapboard house on the edge of town. I had always lived in a public building—the center of the community—so a private residence was a new experience. After the rest of the family arrived, we settled in the rental house and soon discovered ways to entertain ourselves. The restaurant at the nearby hotel featured a pianist, and we loved to eat a meal while listening to her play music from the 1920s and 30s.

I will never forget the time that I saw my first cow. People might wonder why a cow made such an impression on me, since I had seen many more exotic animals, such as moose, caribou, and reindeer. Possibly the way that I was introduced to the cow made it a memorable experience. We were eating dinner at the hotel restaurant when we heard a very loud sound that startled all of us. I was terrified. Our table was next to an open window. An old cow stuck her head in the window above my head and let out a loud, bellowing moo. I had no idea what kind of animal it was, but when the other people in the room started laughing, I realized that the creature did not intend to have me for dinner.

In one of the stores we saw our first canvas shoes. We had only known mukluks and rubber boots so, of course, we each had to have a pair of those new shoes. With our new white Converse high-tops neatly laced, we stepped out of the store onto the boarded sidewalk. We had come a long way from Selawik. We continued our stroll down the street, never taking our eyes off our feet.

After we were settled in the house in Ruby, Dad went on to Poorman to make the Roadhouse ready for the family, leaving us to enjoy "big city" life. After several days, I missed my dad and began to beg Mom to allow me to go see him. This went on for days, until Mom, needing a much-deserved break from my incessant pleading, made arrangements for me to travel to Poorman with an old Norwegian miner named Mr. Knutson. Mr. Knutson and I climbed into a mule-driven wagon to begin our sixty-mile journey to Poorman. As we pulled away from the clapboard house in Ruby, I remember my mom standing on the porch in her calico dress and apron, waving good-bye with her handkerchief.

Poorman was sixty miles south down a poorly graded dirt road. Thirty miles was a full day in a mule-drawn wagon, so we stopped in Long Creek, a mining town halfway between Ruby and Poorman. Mr. Knutson had some friends there who were kind enough to offer us something to eat and a place to stay. Late the next afternoon, we arrived in Poorman and drove straight to Dad's new store, the Roadhouse. I could see the Roadhouse way up ahead of the team, and I strained to see Dad. I was also straining to see what my new living quarters were like. From that distance, it wasn't very impressive, and it only looked worse as we drew closer. As we pulled up to the building, Dad came out to greet us. "Well, Audrey, what do you think of your new home?" I did not say it, but my first thought was that Mom was not going to like the place. At ten years of age, I did not know much about what a house should look like, but I remember thinking that the building looked ugly with black tar paper covering the outside. Did someone forget to put the siding on? At that particular moment, however, the most important thing was that I was with my dad, and I hugged him, keeping my initial thoughts to myself.

Dad gave me a tour of the Roadhouse, first presenting the general store, post office, and kitchen downstairs. The store was at one end of the building and had a large wooden counter and glass display case. The case contained a grand assortment of supplies—everything the traveler or miner might need. Barrels of various sizes were everywhere, and I remember thinking that it was going to be fun to explore what was inside of them. Our living quarters were upstairs and included a large living room and four bedrooms. As with most residences in Alaska, plumbing was nonexistent and the bathroom facilities were "out back," but for the very first time we had electricity from a generator.

Dad was very excited about the Roadhouse and was proud to be a storeowner and the postmaster of Poorman. After showing me around the store and living quarters, Dad said that it was time for bed. At those words, loneliness for my mom engulfed me and I began to cry. All I could see was my mom standing on the porch in her calico dress and apron, waving good-bye with her handkerchief. I cried half the night. Poor Dad. He had no idea how to console me. Exercising his authority as the new postmaster of Poorman, Dad decided to return me "to sender."

The next morning, tired, red-faced, and puffy-eyed, I climbed into a wagon with Lars Olson, another miner who was instructed to take me back to Ruby. My big adventure in Poorman lasted less than twenty-four hours. A few weeks later, Dad sent for all of us and we began our new lives in the mining camp.

POORMAN AND THE ROADHOUSE

LIFE IN THE INTERIOR OF ALASKA WAS VERY DIFFERENT than our experience north of the Arctic Circle; one of the only similarities was that our family's home was again the central point of activity in the community. The terrain consisted of mainly tundra, the mounds of soft, spongy grass that made walking in a straight line virtually impossible. We had tundra surrounding Selawik; however, now the tundra was dotted with clumps of trees and large bushes. This land had a charm all its own. There were numerous creeks surrounding Poorman that were frequented by the gold-seekers, but there was no large river as in Selawik.

I often pondered my dad's decision to leave Selawik and move to Poorman. Commercialism, free enterprise, his desire to take an active part in the frontier economy—these factors may have played a role; however, I am now convinced that the main reason was the hope of providing more financially for his family.

The Roadhouse at Poorman, Alaska, 1937.

Gone were the days of summer vacations, as Dad was committed to the store and available to the miners every day, twenty-four hours a day. He spent most of his days in the Roadhouse, making sales and handling the mail service. Behind the counter were rows of canned goods, tins of coffee, spools of twine, first-aid items, and the post office mailboxes. Essentials for miners, such as Eveready flashlights and batteries, lined the top of the long wooden counter. Fifty-pound sacks of flour, sugar, and beans were stacked in one corner of the room. Tools of the trade—picks, shovels, saws, axes, and shiny, round gold pans were displayed on one wall of the store. Supplies for the store came on wagons pulled by teams of mules up the dirt road from Ruby to Poorman.

The centerpiece of Dad's store was the brass scale for weighing the gold that the miners brought in. It was a very fine and beautiful piece, even though it seemed like an antique even then. Dad was very proud of it, and we were not to touch it. The scale must have had the precision of a fine watch because Dad used it to carefully weigh the gold, exactly calculating to the tenth of an ounce. This scale was important to the entire economy since most of the miners paid for their goods from their moose-hide pokes filled with gold dust and nuggets. Dad owned a few buildings across the road that he used as warehouses for storing goods. He also dug a deep hole for cold storage. Fresh and frozen meats were stored at the bottom of the hole, which Dad accessed by climbing down a wooden ladder. He loved bacon and eggs, and once a year he would order large slabs of bacon that were kept in the cold storage. Many times, I watched Dad scrape green mold off the outside of the slab and cut thick slices of bacon for the next meal.

Dad regularly ordered candy—chocolate-covered bonbons with pink or white filling that he sold by the pound. I would often slip behind the counter, and years later he told me that when he opened the boxes of candy, there would be a candy out of every box. Some candy came in bulk—the old-fashioned crème drops that come in packages today came in bulk in a basket with a lid. Sold by the pound for ten cents per pound, these were called "ten-cent chocolates."

Irus in the general store at the Roadhouse.

According to territorial law, hard liquor had to be locked up in a warehouse, away from the store. Possibly due to my craving for sweets, Dad decided the only safe place for the candy was to be locked up with the liquor behind the mesh chicken wire fence. However, I always found the chocolate hidden behind the counter when he was not in the store.

The Roadhouse was the community center, and every evening the miners came to sit, visit, and play cards. I'm sure they also came for the beer since Dad's beer cellar was right under the pan table (pan is a card game similar to poker). While in bed at night, I often heard the table scraping across the wood floor, revealing the trap door. Then, I would hear Dad's boots going down the ladder to retrieve cold beer for the miners.

Mom was never happy about the beer drinking, which sometimes lasted late into the night. From my bed, I could hear the clicking of the chips as they were stacked and moved on the pan table. About one hundred men lived in the camp, and we had many men in the Roadhouse on any given evening. A few women lived in Poorman and worked as cooks at the surrounding mining sites. Most of the miners owned their own cabins, but many would come and go. Almost all were single, so their entertainment consisted of "hanging out" at the Roadhouse every evening.

One of Dad's prospecting associates, Baldo Forno, liked to come over every night around eight o'clock when most of the other miners were leaving. Baldo loved to talk and he usually stayed for hours discussing mining issues with Dad. Mom started turning the lights off before Baldo got there, hoping he would be deterred from coming into the Road-house. I always wanted Mom to be nice to Baldo, as he had a horse that he would sometimes let me ride.

Occasionally, when the miners were in the Roadhouse during the evening, one of the miners would shout, "Wind up the Victrola!"…and the dance would begin. Card playing was temporarily halted as the tables and chairs were shoved across the wooden floor to the sides of the room. Every miner thought he knew how to dance, and some of them did. A large number of Scandinavians lived in the camp, and they loved to dance the polka and the shottish. I became a pretty good dancer because when it came time to grab a dance partner, I was one of the few available females. I don't think it was because I was especially pretty, since Dave had as many offers to dance as I did.

While Dad managed the Roadhouse store and community center, Mom ran the Cookhouse in the back part of the building. Miners loved to dance, but they especially loved to eat. The kitchen was quite large and had a long wooden plank dining table that spanned half the length of the room. There was also a small living area off to the side just large enough for two chairs separated by a lamp table. As in Selawik, a water barrel stood in the kitchen. Running water did not exist in Poorman, so during the summer all water was carried in from the pump. During the winter, our water source was melted snow. The back door led outside to the outhouse and the can pile (garbage). Thinking back on those years in Poorman, I often wonder how my mother did what she did. Rising early in the morning, she began her day by making breakfast for us, as well as any miners who were staying in the small bunkhouse off the kitchen. After washing pots and pans and cleaning up after breakfast, it was time to start lunch. Mom's routine continued through dinner. Any visitors to the camp who needed a meal could find satisfaction at the Cookhouse any time of the day. A sign on the wall stated "Welcome. One dollar per meal."

———

We all have certain regrets about how we behaved in a situation from our past, and one of mine involves my years in Poorman. Like most children, I disliked helping with the dishes. In fact, I disliked any kind of chores. At ten or eleven years old, my mission in life was to play. When it was time to do the dishes in the Cookhouse, I usually headed for the outhouse. A small hole in the outhouse door enabled me to have full view of the back kitchen door and the nearby clothesline. When Mom came out of the door and headed for the clothesline to hang the damp dishtowels, I knew it was safe to emerge. In later years, my guilt was heavy when I recalled her difficult life in Poorman. I could not do enough for my mom to try and make up for my bad behavior.

"Big 'n Tuff" Audrey at the Roadhouse.

Besides cooking three meals a day for the family and the miners, Mom cooked several loaves of bread and sold them for fifteen cents a loaf. Most of the bread was sourdough bread, made with the sourdough starter that bubbled and fermented in a tin can on the kitchen table. Although I tried to avoid the meal clean-up process, rarely did I miss a meal (or an unsold loaf of bread). As a result, I gained weight quickly, and by the age of eleven, I was much larger than my petite mother. I had long, straight blonde hair and wore overalls. I called myself "big and tough" and prided myself on being a tomboy. (I was unaware that while I was pleased with my transformation into a big and tough tomboy, my older sisters were transforming their images according to the current styles in the States. They were turning into beautiful ladies.)

Electricity from the generator meant that we could have a real radio. The large brown radio with the round top and cloth speaker in the middle was Gramps's pride and joy. Gramps loved the radio. He listened to all sorts of programs, and I remember he especially liked to listen to the Joe Louis fights. He was hard of hearing, and when he was listening to a fight, we had to be silent in the house so he could hear it. We never missed *The Al Jolson Show* and *Fibber McGee and Mollie,* eagerly pulling our chairs up to the table or to a spot near the radio. Although the radio was our main source of entertainment during the coldest winter months, Dave and I spent most of our time out-of-doors.

TENDERFEET AND SOURDOUGHS

THE ROADHOUSE SAT ON A HILL OVERLOOKING A SMALL valley. A narrow dirt road, just wide enough for a mule-drawn wagon, led to the bottom of the hill, and "efficiency" one-room log cabins owned by the miners dotted the sides of the road and the surrounding area. A few tents had been erected between cabins for those unsure of whether they would stay long.

When news arrived in the lower forty-eight about gold discoveries in Alaska, thousands of men and a few hardy women traveled there to seek their fortunes. Almost all were tenderfeet—inexperienced and not used to hardships. Not yet toughened to outdoor life in Alaska, many left after experiencing one brutal winter, unable to cope with the cold, loneliness, and separation from their families. Then, there were those who were diligent in their perseverance, living to tell their story and earning the name "sourdough," the name Alaskans give to those who made it. My dad and many of the miners in Poorman were prime examples of "sourdoughs."

Audrey and the miners

After my sister June left Poorman to attend high school in Seattle, Dave and I were the only children in the camp. That made us celebrities of sorts, and the miners were very protective of us. Mom and Dad trusted them to be around us. Other than the drinking and card playing at the Roadhouse, the men were very careful with their conduct and tried their best not to swear when we were around.

Very few women lived in Poorman. Some were wives of miners, although most wives did not travel to the North Country with their fortune-seeking husbands. Several women worked as cooks in the surrounding mining camps. The only other reason for a woman to be in Poorman was to provide entertainment for the men. These women came from the "lower forty-eight," as well as from other countries, and lived alone in single-room cabins. This included the lady who lived across the road from us.

Everyone who searched for gold hoped to get rich. Most of the miners worked independently, panning for gold in the creeks around the camps at Poorman, Long Creek, and Ruby. They kept the success or failure of their mining efforts a closely guarded secret. It seemed like they wanted everyone to think the only thing they were finding was just more gravel. In the case of a "strike," the miner immediately rushed to file a claim with Dad. After filling out the necessary paperwork, Dad sent the claim papers directly to Juneau. Then the miner would buy more supplies before returning to work his promising new claim.

The Poorman area was well known for placer mining, and mining equipment was set up in and all around the camp. "Placer" comes from a Spanish word meaning "sand banks." I spent many hours watching the miners dig deep holes in the ground and haul up buckets of soil, depositing the "pay dirt" into huge piles. Then, they pushed the dirt into wooden sluice boxes, set at an angle, and washed it with water. The sluice box was a long wooden channel with "riffles," or slats, nailed in the bottom to catch gold. As the water ran through the box, it washed away the lighter gravel, but the gold was trapped in the riffles. The favorite point in the process, "clean-up," began when the miner stopped the water and searched for gold flakes and nuggets at the bottom of the sluice box. When the water receded, tiny nuggets and flakes of gold could be seen trapped between the riffles nailed across the bottom of the box. Occasionally, one of the local miners let me feel around in the gravel and sand for gold nuggets before the water completely drained from the sluice box. Sometimes a miner asked me to hold the long sealskin or moose-hide poke while he dropped the gold into it. He then set the drawstring tight, tucking the poke into his coat until he could take it to my dad at the Roadhouse for weighing in.

Many of the miners left Poorman for weeks and months at a time to follow leads. These seasoned old sourdoughs would leave the camp in any season, undeterred by the weather conditions. All along the Yukon River and the mining trails, miners had erected small cabins that were available to any traveling prospector. The unspoken rules included:

Take care of the property, replace what you use, and leave an extra something for the next traveler. For summertime travelers, the cabins offered welcomed protection from the swarming mosquitoes along the trail.

Dad loved to tell us his frozen fly story. On one of his many trips into the wilderness of northern Alaska during the winter, Dad found an available miner's cabin at the end of the day and immediately started a fire in the woodstove. As the cabin began to warm, Dad unpacked his dinner and settled in for the night. He had brought his favorite bread, corndodgers—cornbread cooked hard, cut into squares, and perfect for dipping into maple syrup. Warming the syrup over the fire turned the corndodgers into an extraordinary treat. *Buzz… Buzz…* What was that? At forty below zero, how could any living thing survive in a cabin heated only when a prospector visits for a night? Especially an insect! *Buzz… Buzz…* A fly landed on Dad's pan of beans and cornbread. Then, another fly came buzzing by. Within minutes, hundreds of flies were dive-bombing Dad's dinner and swarming in the tiny space.

Dad threw open the cabin door and shooed the flies outside by wildly waving a pair of long underwear from his pack, sending the flies to an immediate death. The flies had been frozen on the ceiling of the cabin, and as the stove warmed the small space, the flies came to life, thankful for a second chance at living. Dad was always puzzled that the flies could not survive outside, yet could survive in a frozen state on the ceiling of the cabin. Only in Alaska.

Besides corndodgers, another staple of the prospector's life was sourdough bread. Many miners carried their sourdough starter and a sack of flour with them when traveling. At any time, fresh bread could be had when on the mining trails. The starter would die if it froze, so most of the miners carried it in a container in their parka and slept with it at night to keep the valuable mixture warm.

Like the Alaskan natives, visitors to this part of the world figured out how to survive.

FINNELLIE AND
THE EXPLOSION

ELLIE WAS A SINGLE LADY FROM FINLAND WHO LIVED IN a small log cabin across the road from us. My brother and I began calling her FinnEllie, and soon everyone in Poorman called her by that name. She looked like the other women in the camp—calico dress, apron, nothing to set her apart from the rest.

FinnEllie was nice to Dave and me, and Mom would often tell us, "Be kind to FinnEllie and always show her respect." Our mother treated all people with kindness and respect, and we were taught to do the same, so these words were not unusual coming from her. Once or twice she added an additional sentence, "I do not like what FinnEllie does, but I love her gentle, thoughtful spirit." We didn't waste any time wondering what she did. We thought she was probably a cook in the camp. One day, my parents decided to go for a walk on the dirt roads around Poorman. This was a rare activity for them—to get away from the Roadhouse for even a few moments alone. Dave and I received our instructions to stay close to the Roadhouse and not get into any trouble. Like most nine- and eleven-year-olds, we soon became bored with just sitting around, "not getting into any trouble."

I don't know which one of us thought of the idea first,

but we decided to start dinner as a surprise for our parents. Starting dinner meant lighting the stove, so we discussed this procedure, although not in much detail. Together, we gathered wood from the woodpile outside the kitchen door and packed it into the big black stove. Dave announced that he knew how Dad lit the fire and took off to one of the storage buildings across the road to obtain the "magic" lighting fluid.

When Dave returned, he was holding a Hills Brothers coffee can full of liquid. "Coal oil," he said, smiling broadly, obviously extremely proud of his achievement. Dave tossed the smelly liquid onto the wood, and I quickly threw a lighted match into the stove. The explosion was immediate—Boom! The Roadhouse walls shook. The lid on the stove blew off as if shot from a canon, hitting the opposite wall and crashing to the ground. Ashes resembling gray snow flurries flew all over the kitchen and settled on our hair, arms, and clothing. Dave and I were sure we had been killed. Our wide eyes found one another through the haze as clouds of black smoke poured out of the stove door and filled the cabin.

Realizing we were still alive, our ears ringing, we ran out the door and across the road to FinnEllie's house. (Fortunately, she was not working that day.) We fell upon her cabin door, our fists pounding loudly. With one look at her blackened and frightened young neighbors, FinnEllie wrapped her arms around us, trying to make sense of our broken words amidst the wheezing. She understood "Fire!" and "Boom!" and hurried with us back to the Roadhouse to evaluate the damage. Fortunately, the Roadhouse was still standing and was not on fire. FinnEllie helped us sweep the ashes and clean up the mess. I don't recall how my parents responded to our story of tossing gasoline into the stove, but maybe it is better that way. We were just glad that we were not dead.

A few months later, FinnEllie moved out of Poorman.

Like many women in her situation, she left without telling anyone where she was going. Sometime after FinnEllie's departure, Mom and I traveled to Ruby by wagon to purchase supplies for the Roadhouse. While walking down the main street, we heard a familiar voice call, "Mrs. Purkeypile! Mrs. Purkeypile!" We turned to see FinnEllie waving to us and walking across the street to greet us. "Mrs. Purkeypile, would you join me at my house for tea?" Without hesitation, my mother's answer was, "Certainly!" and off we went to her new home.

FinnEllie lived in a small log cabin off the main dirt road in Ruby. The cabin was neat, clean, and well lit; flowered curtains on the windows were open, allowing the sunshine to warm the room. Simply furnished, the cabin living area had two upholstered chairs with a small round table in between. A small kerosene lamp and a Bible were on the table atop a crocheted lace doily. Mom and FinnEllie sat in the chairs, sipping on their tea. I sat on the floor at Mom's feet.

FinnEllie asked about Dad and Dave and the rest of the family. She became momentarily quiet, as if carefully forming her next words.

"Mrs. Purkeypile, I want you to know something. I no longer do what I used to do. I am a changed woman."

Mom reached over and gently laid her hand on FinnEllie's hand. Nothing else needed to be said. Years later, when pondering our relationship with FinnEllie, I was convinced that her transformation was a direct result of my mother's continual commitment to always treat this woman with kindness and respect.

POORMAN PLAY

SINCE DAVE AND I WERE THE ONLY CHILDREN IN POOR-man, school was held at the kitchen table in the Cookhouse. After settling in our new home, I began fifth grade with the Calvert Course from the University of Maryland. Dave and I would start school immediately following breakfast and our regular chores. Mom was very strict about our educa-tion; fortunately for her, I was a very good student and loved to study. Dave, on the other hand, was not a fan of school and much preferred to play. Only two events could excuse us from our studies—if Scotty came with the mail or if an airplane landed on the air strip.

Airplanes came into Poorman for a variety of reasons, but usually to deliver mail, supplies, or to transport miners. The second we heard an airplane in the distance, the begging would commence. "Mom, an airplane! Can we go, *please?*" After receiving permission to leave the house, Dave and I bolted out the kitchen door and scrambled up the hill to the airstrip. Even before he became a legendary bush pilot, Jim Dodson was one of our favorites, and we were always excited when we recognized his familiar plane. We loved to hear his stories, especially the one about an accident he survived. (All of the bush pilots had stories about crashing airplanes and survival, and Mr. Dodson was no different.) In this par-ticular story, Mr. Dodson crashed his plane on a river bed and sustained a broken leg. With one working leg and in excruciating pain, he managed to remove a pontoon from the plane and use it as a kayak to float down the river for help. Dave and I never tired of hearing the pilots tell about their adventures.

Scotty the Mailman lived in Ruby and delivered mail to the surrounding mining camps and villages. He pulled into Poorman about every two weeks, driving his sled with as many as twenty dogs. Working at the kitchen table on schoolwork, I would hear the door to the Roadhouse open and bang shut. "Hello, Irus! Where's my assistant?" With those words, Mom would nod her head before my words were formed.

"Come on, Audrey! We're tired, cold, and hungry!" Scotty let me help him unhook the dogs and lead them into a large barn that stood about halfway down the hill from the Roadhouse. The dogs were fed dried fish and cull meat from moose, bear, and reindeer; these were kept in "cold storage," a hole dug in the ground next to the barn. Scotty usually came with fifteen to twenty malamutes, large dogs descended from Arctic wolves, so caring for the dogs took the majority of the day. After feeding, the dogs lay down on the barn floor, and I brushed each one, calling them by name and filling them in on the Poorman news. Their muzzles and legs were snow white and their eyes a deep brown, surrounded with what appeared to be black eyeliner. They seemed to understand my newsy chatter and to appreciate the attention.

Sometime prior to my eleventh birthday, my parents revealed the promise of a birthday gift to come—a large doll ordered from the Sears catalogue. After the doll arrived by ship to Ruby, Scotty would deliver the doll to me in Poorman. A week or so later when I heard Scotty and the team pull in front of the Roadhouse, I was out the door in a flash.

"Scotty, do you have a package for me?"

"Well, Audrey, why don't you look under those furs in the sled?"

Tucked into the sled, under a pile of beaver pelts and caribou and moose hides, was the biggest doll I had ever laid eyes on. She might not have been the most beautiful, but she was definitely the largest—almost three feet tall. Since I was the only young girl in Poorman, Patty became my new best friend.

Patty and I spent hours playing on the tundra. In our play world, we kept house, hunted animals, fished, looked for gold, and talked about life. When I sat, Patty sat beside me. When I stood up, Patty stood up beside me, holding my hand.

A large Swedish woman, the wife of a miner, lived in a cabin next to the Roadhouse. From her cabin window, Mrs. Johnson had a perfect view of the tundra. I will not say that she was a nosy neighbor, but she was committed to looking out for Dave and me, as were most of the residents of Poorman. One day, Mrs. Johnson watched Patty and me playing on the soft, spongy mounds of grass and wondered who the new child in Poorman might be. The next time she went into the Roadhouse, she asked, "Who is Audrey's company?" My dad laughed so hard that he wiped tears from his face. Mrs. Johnson was quite surprised to learn that my "company" was a doll.

After caring for Scotty's sled dog team for several months, I decided that Dave and I should start building our own team. Most of the working dogs in Alaska were true Siberian huskies and malamutes, but our dog team was going to be different. I think Dave and I pioneered the idea of a dog-rescue mission. During the time we lived in Poorman, we "acquired" dogs and eventually formed a small sled dog team of our own. Miners often offered us puppies from their dogs' litters, and occasionally a traveler left a dog in the camp. At one time we had nine dogs chained to wooden poles next to doghouses in back of the Roadhouse. Some appeared worthy of the title "sled dog," but most were of questionable parentage.

We had a large wolf-dog we called Rex. He was a good sled dog, but he was very nervous. Every so often we had to replace his pole, as he ran round and round on his chain and would wear it out. Trixie, the lead dog, gave us several litters of pups, and we always kept at least one puppy. As all children do with new puppies, Dave and I named them all and begged to keep some to raise; Buck, Bingo, and Nippie were three of our favorites. We fed our dogs hot oatmeal and dried fish. Mom let us use her big Dutch oven, and we cooked large batches of oatmeal at a time. Our sled was donated to us by a miner who had had enough of mining and was heading home to Oregon. Made of birch wood, the sled had been carefully carved by an Indian in the area. Strips of tin were attached to the runners to increase speed on the ice and snow. Dave and I took every opportunity to drive our rag-tag dog team around to the mining camps surrounding Poorman. We took turns mushing and waving to our friends. "Gee! (left)" and "Haw! (right)" were two of our favorite words and made us (so we thought) look and sound very authentic. Everyone knew Audrey and Dave.

Audrey taking a ride with her sled dog team in Poorman.

I only remember one time when the dogs were used for a purpose. An airplane flipped over onto its back as it was landing on the Poorman airstrip, and all dog teams were summoned to assist with pulling the plane from the runway. The men tied ropes to the tail of the plane and to the sleds. With all the mushers yelling at their dogs, the teams strained and pulled the plane to the side. Dave and I felt that without our team, the effort would not have been a success. We felt quite important.

My brother and I found many other ways to entertain ourselves in Poorman. Dad routinely received large shipments of supplies for the store, so we had a regular supply of the best and most versatile toys a kid could hope for—boxes! In our pursuit of creative ways to have fun with boxes, we learned that Lucky Strike boxes made perfect airplanes. Cut one hole for your head and two holes for your arms (wings) and you have a very airworthy bush plane. After fashioning a plane for each of us, Dave and I would climb into our planes. One of us was always Archie Ferguson and the other was Jim Dodson. With authentic engine sounds and pilot radio communications, we skillfully flew our planes all over the camp. We only stopped flying when we had crashed so many times that our planes were no longer airworthy—or Mom called us in for dinner. Somehow we thought that crashing our planes was an essential part of being a bush pilot.

Dave, the bush pilot.

Winter in Poorman was very cold with large accumulations of snow and drifts; however, the days were longer than in Selawik. More daylight hours enabled us to spend time cross-country skiing and sledding when not in school. As soon as the ground thawed, Dave and I planted and tended vegetable gardens, enjoying bumper crops as a result of the long hours of summer sun. We tended the garden daily; cabbage, turnips, carrots, and tomatoes grew well there. Berries were plentiful in the surrounding tundra. Occasionally, a hunter would bring us a duck or goose for a rare treat. What could be better than roast wild duck with fresh vegetables and fresh berries? Picking berries and plucking ducks was our specialty; cooking was not. We counted on Mom to turn our prizes into something edible.

Although we were best friends and played together all the time, Dave and I did our share of bickering and arguing. Sometimes verbal fighting turned into a good old rolling-around-the-yard physical fight. Since I was much larger than Dave and outweighed him by perhaps twenty or thirty pounds, I could usually gain the advantage. The fight often ended with me sitting on top of him. He would get so mad, I thought he might explode. I was delighted! Sometimes, I relinquished my perch upon gaining some concession from Dave, but usually it was when I heard Mom yell, "Audrey Davine Purkeypile!" Mom was the gentlest person I have ever known, but occasionally she would have enough of the squawking and discord. I will never forget the time she took after us with a broom and chased us around the kitchen table and out the door. This was also one of those "full-name" occasions.

One year, our parents ordered two bicycles from Sears for our birthdays. The rutted dirt roads of the camp that had been the airstrips for our cardboard box bush planes became our racetrack. Dave and I were already popular with the miners, but we became more so after the bikes arrived. Miners raced miners, miners raced one of us, and Dave and I raced each other. We never went anywhere on the bikes without racing, so everyone in the camp knew it would happen sooner or later—and it did. One particular contest ended at the bottom of the hill with a spectacular collision. Dave somehow emerged unscathed, but my knee was cut badly and needed medical attention. Dad enlisted the services of a visiting dentist who sewed several stitches to close the wound. The dentist, a known alcoholic, provided no anesthetic, so I remember the experience well. When purchasing medical services with canned goods, the quality of the service can be limited.

Occasionally around Poorman, Dave and I came across an old abandoned gold-mining rocker. The rockers actually looked like rockers—wooden bucket affairs on skids with handles. Piles of rock and dirt that had already been sifted, called tailings, were piled in high mounds next to the rocker. Convinced that the miners had missed some large chunks of gold, Dave and I would spend hours putting the dirt back into the rockers and searching for the lost nuggets. Sometimes the repeat "clean-up" proved profitable and, after running water over the dirt in the mesh tray, we discovered some gold dust that had fallen to the bottom. We put our gold dust into a small glass vial and proudly showed our newly found wealth to the miners in the camp. All of our miner friends at least pretended to be very pleased with our good fortune.

Audrey and Dave heading to the creek to pan for gold.

My sister Mimi came back to Alaska in 1938 and joined us in Poorman. We had not seen her for the four years she was in Seattle. Mimi arrived at the airstrip, traveling from

Fairbanks to Poorman with Jim Dodson. When Dave and I saw her, we were starstruck. We simply did not recognize her. Where was "the boss," the captain of the "football team"? Where was the one who could outrun and outshoot all of her friends and hunt down muskrats with the best of the Eskimo hunters? Where was the girl with long hair braided down her back like her Eskimo friends? This beautiful lady, with her stylish hair and dress, looked more like a starlet. Until Mimi's return from Seattle, I had been quite pleased with my "big and tough" image. Recognizing the sharp contrast between my appearance and my sister's, I felt pretty silly, sort of like an ugly duckling. I pondered this for a short time, but then Dave wanted to play, and the call to be a kid was much stronger than the desire to grow up.

Mimi lived with us for a short time, helping Mom in the Cookhouse, but soon began cooking in one of the nearby camps. Norma returned from Seattle following her high school graduation and immediately became Mom's right hand in the kitchen. Norma had always been comfortable in the kitchen and was an excellent cook. Both of my sisters were courted by young miners, and they soon married, again changing our family structure.

With the coming and going of the sisters, Dave and I thought it our duty to "hold down the fort" in Poorman. We continued to play with our dogs, spend time panning for gold, and enjoy our life with the miners. The thought of growing up was not forefront in my mind, but reality would soon be upon me. My life was about to change.

THE OUTSIDE

DURING THE 1939–40 SCHOOL YEAR, I FINISHED BOTH seventh- and eighth-grade curriculum, completing my work at our school, the kitchen table in the Cookhouse. My parents decided that Audrey, at the age of thirteen, was ready to go to "the outside." At that time, I wasn't ready to go anywhere and would have agreed to anything to be able to stay in Alaska, even if it meant repeating the seventh and eighth grades.

In the fall of 1940, the decision was made, and Mom and Dad made arrangements for me to join my sister June in Seattle. I would attend Franklin High School, the same school that June attended. Since Mimi and Norma had returned to Alaska, Auntie Jennie had additional room in her home, and she graciously agreed to have me stay there with June.

One of my mother's friends was sending her daughter to a private school in Seattle, and Mom made arrangements for me to travel with her. My "chaperone" was only fifteen herself, but she was definitely wiser in the ways of the world than I was. Whatever age she was, I was just glad to have someone travel with me.

The first leg of my trip was a flight from Poorman to Fairbanks, where I would meet my chaperone. Dave and I were usually racing up the hill to the airstrip to greet any arriving plane, but on this occasion we walked slowly. Mom, Dad, Mimi, and Norma walked with us. For the first time in my life, I was moving away from my family. Jim Dodson's familiar face greeted us at his plane. I hugged each family member over and over again until Mr. Dodson said we needed to leave and helped me climb into the plane for the flight. As we lifted off, I pressed my face against the window and watched my family fade into the distance. Mom never stopped waving with her white handkerchief, the one with the purple pansies embroidered in the corner.

Denise Coyle and her parents met me at the Fairbanks Airport and took me to their home for the night. That evening, Denise wanted to show me the sights of the big city; we walked to the Lacy Theater to see a movie. I don't remember the title, but I do remember that three or four minutes passed before I realized the movie had sound. "Denise! They're talking!" She probably did not know what to make of this girl from the backwoods. The only "movie" I had ever seen was an eight-millimeter cartoon at Archie Ferguson's home in Kotzebue.

I had never been anywhere in my life except for Eskimo villages and mining camps. Although Fairbanks was a small town at that time, it was a big city to me. My time of enlightenment and exploration in Fairbanks was limited, however, as we were scheduled to fly to Juneau the following morning.

The only sight I remember on the flight to Juneau was Mt. McKinley looming outside of the plane window. I would like to say that I have more memories of the flight, but they have escaped me. Flying over the glaciers affords passengers spectacular scenery that I have enjoyed a number of times since. However, that day I was only focused on the inside of the airplane and the uncertainty of my future. After arriving in Juneau, we walked to the ship docks to board the *Princess Louise*, a Canadian steamship bound for Seattle. Our mothers had arranged for us to share a small stateroom, and we quickly settled in for the five-day journey.

Along the way, the ship stopped numerous times to unload and load passengers and cargo. When we arrived in Vancouver, British Columbia, a ship official came to our stateroom and announced that I would be escorted from the ship and taken to the American Immigration Office. Someone had alerted them that I did not have any identification, so I could not prove the information on my form allowing entrance to the United States. Mom had failed to give me my birth certificate, and there was no way to prove who I was. I was short and heavy with long blonde hair braided and wound across the top of my head, like the Scandinavian women in Alaska. My calico dress, long black stockings, and white high-top canvas shoes were acceptable, except for one factor—for a few weeks I had been nursing an ingrown toenail and Mom had cut the toe out of one of the shoes, exposing the black stocking.

Leaving the ship with a stranger was terrifying, but walking into the immigration official's office was more so. Never will I forget the man who sat on the other side of the huge wooden desk. For a few moments that seemed like hours, the man looked at me from the top of my braided head to my altered white high-top tennis shoes.

"I am going to ask you some questions," he said slowly. "Who is the president of the United States?"

"Roosevelt." I was not sure sound would come from my mouth, but it did.

"How many states are in the United States?"

"Forty-eight."

"Where is the Empire State Building?"

"New York City."

The man paused, eyeing me and seemingly wondering

how a young girl from Europe would know this information. His lips curled slightly into a small, knowing smile.

"How many red stripes and how many white stripes are on the American flag?"

With that question, I thought my heart would stop. Dad had taught me U.S. history in Selawik, and we studied the flag's design, but I had no idea how many red and white stripes were on that flag. The stress of the past few hours overtook me and the flood of tears started. With my head in my hands, I sobbed loudly. "I don't know, I don't know!"

In all of this man's training as an immigration officer, he must not have learned how to stand up to a sobbing teenage girl. Thankfully, he felt compassion for me and decided to believe my story. He called the man who had delivered me to the immigration office and instructed him to return me to the ship.

Here is a fact that I will never forget—there are thirteen total stripes on the American flag. Seven red stripes and six white stripes give honor to the thirteen original colonies.

When the *Princess Louise* docked in Seattle, my sister June and Auntie Jennie were standing on the dock, waving and calling my name. We boarded a bus to travel to Auntie Jennie's house, and I experienced my first bus ride. As we drove through Seattle, my neck became stiff from straining to look up at the tall buildings, including the Smith Tower, the tallest building at that time in the western United States.

Amazingly enough, I adjusted fairly quickly to my new life in the big city. The small house off Ranier Avenue housed Auntie Jennie, her two daughters, and two grandsons. With the Purkeypile girls added to the mix, quarters were tight, but Auntie treated us as her daughters.

June and I received a weekly allowance of fifteen cents, and the money burned a hole in our pockets until we could spend it. Each week after receiving our allowance, we walked down Rainier Avenue to the movie theater. Auntie often took us with her on the bus for the weekly shopping excursion to Pikes Market. The main attraction for me was the escalator in the nearby JCPenney store, an experience not found in Alaska. As my reward for helping with the shopping, Auntie often gave me ten cents to purchase soft ice cream in the basement. The frozen treat was swirled into a tall glass and eaten with a long spoon. On Auntie's shopping day, I was usually the first one with a hand up, volunteering my services.

In spite of the occasional trips to the soda fountain, I lost almost thirty pounds during my months with Auntie. She closely monitored my food intake and usually did not allow snacking between meals. Often, she said that she wanted to put a sign over her door: Auntie's Diet House.

The greatest adjustment to Franklin High School was being around so many other students. My school experiences had included Alaska government school with Eskimo children and home school with my brother, Dave. June and I rode the bus together every day, but as soon as we arrived at the school, I was on my own until we met at the end of the day. Academically, my education in Selawik and Poorman had been excellent, and I was well prepared for school, learned quickly, and made good grades.

Many sights and experiences were new and exciting in Seattle, but one of the best was my first ride in an automobile. I was a bit of a novelty at school, and the Franklin High School newspaper published the following article during my first year there...

ALASKA GIRLS HAVE FIRST RIDE IN SEATTLE

Imagine living in a remote Eskimo village in Alaska, eating whale and seal meat, and playing with Eskimos? "That would be awful," you might think, but June and Audrey Purkeypile, junior and freshman, respectively, lived that way until this fall and liked it.

This is Audrey's first trip outside of Alaska, for she was born in the Arctic Circle and has lived in Alaska all her life.

It must have seemed like another world to Audrey when she arrived in Seattle last summer to attend high school, for you do not see trains, steamers, and tall apartment buildings in northern Alaska. Audrey rode in an automobile for the first time in her life when she came to Seattle. Dog teams had furnished the only means of transportation in her former home.

Audrey's father and mother taught in a government school in an Eskimo village where they were the only white family. When Audrey was ten, her family moved to Poorman, the lonely mining camp that was her home until this summer. Her father keeps a combination store and roadhouse in the camp.

Audrey likes Seattle very much, but she can hardly wait to return to her home in Alaska.

During the summer of 1941, June and I gave our Auntie a break, spending the summer in British Columbia with relatives. Reminiscent of our summers in Selawik, those two months were filled with swimming, camping, and singing with cousins whom we had never met before that time. I know my mother was happy for us, but knew how much she would have loved to be with us that summer.

This was the summer before life in America would change forever.

THE WAR YEARS

AT THE END OF THE SUMMER OF 1941, JUNE AND I TRAV-
eled back to Seattle for another year of school. June was in
her senior year, and I was fourteen and a sophomore. The
first semester was uneventful, and school was going well for
both of us.

I recall the day when June and I learned that Pearl Harbor had been attacked. On December 7, 1941, June and I
walked down Ranier Avenue to the movie theater. When
we were at the movies, we saw the newsreels and knew there
was war in Europe. Terrible things were happening there,
but the devastation seemed so far away. *One Night in Lis-
bon* was playing, a movie set in London during the war in
Europe starring Fred MacMurray.

On the way home, we talked about the fact that the
newsreels and the movie were all about war. When we walked
into Auntie Jennie's house, we knew immediately that something was wrong. Auntie's face was filled with sadness and
fear. As we sat in her living room, she began to explain to us
what she knew about the attack on Pearl Harbor. She also
told us that President Roosevelt had declared war on Japan.
World War II had begun.

I was only a teenager, but I remember being amazed
at how the people of Seattle and the entire country came
together to sacrifice for "the war effort," as we called it.

Everything mobilized so quickly. Within weeks, Auntie was instructing us in the use of the "coupon book." Coupons limited every item we purchased for the next several years. We had coupons for groceries and meat, coupons for clothing, gasoline, and tires. I had moved beyond mukluks, rubber boots, and high-topped tennis shoes, and I loved shoes. But now every American was limited to purchasing just one pair of shoes per year. Silk stockings were extremely difficult to come by because the silk was being used for parachutes. Women all over the United States saved cans of bacon drippings and donated them to the war effort to use in the manufacture of explosives.

Up and down the blocks, people collected old tires, stacking them into piles on the side of the street for pick-up. Many women in Seattle left their homes early in the morning to work at the naval base at Bremerton, and neighbors helped one another with childcare. The symbol of American women who were working in the factories was Rosie the Riveter, and posters with her picture appeared on windows all over Seattle. Following Pearl Harbor, the Japanese general, Yamamoto, was quoted as saying, "I fear all we have done is to awaken a sleeping giant..." I didn't know if the "giant" had been asleep, but from what I saw from my vantage point in Seattle, Washington, the "giant" was fully awake now.

One day, shortly after the bombing of Pearl Harbor, I went with Auntie Jennie to purchase black broadcloth—yards and yards of black broadcloth. June and I helped her sew the material into blackout curtains for every window in the little house. As soon as the sun began to set and the lights came on in the house, the blackout curtains were pulled tightly.

This nighttime ritual was repeated all over the country, and even Alaska, though seemingly far away, was not exempt. While we were blacking out our windows in Seattle, Dad was performing the job of "war warden" in Poorman. Every day, he patrolled the mining camp to ensure that everyone had their blackout curtains hung and closed during the dark hours, complying with the blackout orders.

Dad was concerned that if the Japanese were to invade Alaska, they would come into our land via Kuskokwim Bay and into the interior up the Kuskokwim River. Most Alaskans had the same fear. The Kuskokwim River was only one hundred fifty miles south of our mining camp in Poorman. A Japanese attack along this route did not occur, although the Japanese did attack Alaska, occupying Attu Island at the far west end of the Aleutians.

Although June and I were probably safer in Seattle than in Poorman, Dad wanted all of his family members back in Alaska to face the future together. So, following June's high school graduation in June 1942, we left Seattle to return to Poorman. We traveled from Seattle to Juneau on one of the princess line ships. Ships were also under blackout orders, a constant reminder of the nearness of the war and the danger of ocean travel during wartime.

When we arrived at the airport in Fairbanks, June and I were greeted by our old friend Jim Dodson, who flew us home. As the plane turned in our approach into Poorman, I could see Dave running up the hill to the airstrip. Mom and Dad were close behind. As soon as the propeller stopped, we were out of the airplane. Everyone started talking at once. Mom, Dad, and Dave all remarked about how much I had changed. Taller and thirty pounds lighter, I am sure that I looked very different. I arrived home feeling like a West Coast young woman who came from a city bustling with streetcars, movie theaters, soldiers, and sailors, where the war was on everyone's mind.

The Purkeypile children in Poorman, 1942.

As I donned my familiar overalls and boots, I was ready to return to the topics of sled dogs and puppies and the best places to pick berries. Although the war was continually on our minds, those summer months in Poorman were filled with swimming, fishing, and berry picking. We invited the young miners to parties and dances at the Roadhouse, again dancing to records played on the old Victrola. I used to get plenty of offers to dance, even in my Big 'n Tuff overalls and high-topped tennis shoes. I now wore a dress for the dances, and with my stylish shoes from Seattle, I felt like the belle of the ball. The language of music always seems to find its way to even remote places, evidenced by the new tunes and latest dances we enjoyed that summer. Several times each week, June, Dave, and I hiked out to the mining camps to visit our old friends. Many were still around, but a few had moved on to other adventures. Toothless Bill had struck it rich, found a wife, and headed back to Oregon. We looked for Mr. and Mrs. Johnson, but heard that they had moved to Seattle. Mr. Johnson had told Dad that he could be poor and starving and freeze to death in Poorman, or he could be just poor and starving in Seattle. Sure that he was going to strike it rich when I left for Seattle, Baldo Forno was still on the verge of striking it rich when I returned. He still had his horse and often let me ride it out to the camps for old times' sake. More than likely, academics did not enter my mind that summer, but my parents were making plans for my continued schooling.

STEP BY STEP

DURING THE SUMMER OF 1942, MOM AND DAD DECIDED to send Dave and me to Fairbanks to complete high school. The U.S. Government intended to suspend all mining operations in Alaska until after the war, greatly affecting my parents' ability to make a living in Poorman. They planned to leave the Roadhouse as soon as possible, but until that time, June, Dave, and I would have to live in Fairbanks alone.

Dad rented us a little log cabin on the Chena River. The cabin was owned by a young man who received the cabin as his inheritance, but was not planning to move into it for several months. Away the three of us went to Fairbanks on our big adventure in September 1942. Mom stayed with us at the cabin for a few weeks until she felt we were settled before returning to Poorman to help Dad. We would not see Mom or Dad for six long months.

> *November 24, 1942*
> *Dear Cousin Alice,*
> *I recently came back from Fairbanks. I was up there for six weeks getting Audrey and Dave started to school. We rented a house and June is with them. Thirteen-year-old David has adjusted himself much more quickly than I had hoped. He is enjoying his first school with other boys. On Saturdays, he works*

at the airport and earns $5.00/day. He loves being around the airplanes.

Audrey is fifteen and in her third year of high school. She is also the housekeeper for the present. June is a stenographer out at Ladd Field and goes to and from work by bus.

Irus and I expect to go up to Fairbanks sometime after Christmas to be with the family. The government passed an order freezing all gold mining for the duration of the war. Our business here depends on the mining, so we have to look for defense work for a while. As soon as we can dispose of our perishable stock, we will board up the Roadhouse until the war is over.

Well, Alice, the Alcan Highway really has been opened. You might have heard the report over the radio. While the war is on, it will be used purely for war purposes, but after peace has come we might be able to visit with each other. It would be a grand trip! We saw the first airplane in Alaska—now the opening of the first land route.

We are having very cold weather tonight—forty degrees below zero. Keeps one busy stoking the fires to keep warm. There is about two feet of snow on the ground. If the family was here, they could have good skiing this winter.

Your cousin,
Ciss

Our new cabin was not particularly roomy, but had sufficient space for the three of us. Dave had his own small bedroom, and June and I shared a room. A window at the back of the house gave us a view of the Chena River and the frequent fishing boats, launches, and planes on pontoons.

The basement housed our heat source, a big, black wood-burning oil drum, as well as numerous pieces of the cabin owner's heirloom furniture. The stair access to the "heater" was under a trapdoor on the floor just inside the front entrance to the cabin. Our pile of wood for cooking and heating the cabin was stacked in back of the cabin. Dave usually started the fire (without gasoline!) when he arrived home from school. In the morning, he started a smaller fire to take the chill off; however, if we were running late for school, we might just hastily throw our clothes on and run out the door.

Each of us had our role in this new family system. June had a good job working at the airbase, so she paid for the cabin rent, all of our food, and other necessities. I was the chief cook and bottle washer but really didn't know how to cook, so our nutritional habits were probably lacking that winter. Our regular daily diet consisted of macaroni and cheese one day and the leftovers the next day. Dave had some assigned chores, but he mainly had fun. Free from Mom and Dad's supervision, his mission was to enjoy his new life with friends his own age. He pursued his mission with tireless energy.

One weekend, Dave and I were anxious for one of our favorite activities—skiing. Recent storms had deposited more than a foot of fresh, powdery snow, and the conditions were perfect. Our problem was that Dave did not have any ski boots. We had all of the equipment except for the boots. We lamented our predicament for a while and then, as a consolation, we decided to eat lunch at a little café that over-looked the Chena River. As we were eating, Dave happened to look on the floor. A folded twenty-dollar bill had been placed under one of the table legs to keep the table from rocking. We could not believe our good fortune. Delivered from our dilemma, we left immediately for the shoe store.

Within the hour, we were skiing down Birch Hill, where the cemetery is today.

A good athlete, Dave had not been exposed to organized team sports, but he found an opportunity to be involved with the athletic events at Fairbanks High School. Dave was one of the guys on the cheerleading squad and attended numerous practices before and after school. Because of Dave's schedule, I usually walked the one and a half miles to and from school alone. Since I was fifteen and concerned with being stylish, I wore skirts, sweaters, and bobby socks but added my ski pants, boots, and fur parka for the long walk. Sometimes the conditions were perfect for ice fog to form. The ice fog would hover just over my head, and although I wrapped a scarf around my face, exposing only my eyes, my eyelashes were frozen with ice by the time I reached the school. Style was nice, but staying warm was more important.

Our first winter in Fairbanks was extremely cold, even for those of us who had lived in the arctic. For weeks, the temperature reached fifty degrees below zero at night. That winter, the woodcutters' union went on strike, and we could not get anyone to help us cut the ten- to twelve-foot logs stacked in back of the cabin. I spent two days walking all over Fairbanks, trying to find someone to help us, but to no avail. As our usable wood dwindled and the temperatures continued to drop, we began to suffer from the cold. At times, the inside thermometer registered twenty degrees when we emerged from under our down quilts in the morning. Our plumbing froze and we were forced to use an old outhouse in a shed behind the cabin. The kitchen woodstove was used very sparingly to save the available cut wood for the heater. For several days, the water in our washbasin was frozen in the morning, and I remember June breaking the ice so she could wash her face before leaving for work.

When our supply of cut wood ran dry, we began to consider our options. The three of us called a family meeting, and after much discussion, deliberation, and shivering, we all came to the same conclusion: Our only option was the wooden furniture in the basement. We proceeded to the basement and solemnly surveyed each item. After debating the merits of each chair, table, desk, and buffet, we agreed upon an oak dining chair with turned legs and a hand-carved back. The three of us vowed that we would be united in the crime together. With a hammer, Dave whacked at the chair legs until the nails loosened and we pulled it apart. June and I stuffed the wood pieces into the oil drum and started the fire while Dave tackled the next chair.

Piece by piece, the furniture kept us warm and alive. Nothing was spared. Over the next few weeks, several chairs, small tables, and a buffet were taken apart and burned. After a time, the furniture in the basement had all turned to ashes. Our situation was still desperate, as the woodcutters remained on strike. We began to see every wooden item in our cabin for its potential as a source of heat. As we prioritized what might end up in the woodstove next, we had a decision to make—burn the chairs, table, and beds upstairs, or start on the wooden steps leading to the basement. The plan soon formed: Pull the wood plank from every other step. That way, we could still get down to the heating drum. Dave and I started at the bottom of the stairs and pulled the first step apart. When that step was turned to ashes, we pulled the step third from the bottom. Then, the fifth from the bottom. Day by day, step by step, we stayed alive.

Prior to starting on the upstairs furniture, I was able to find a man in town who agreed to saw some of our logs for us, and the rest of the winter was uneventful. We never told our parents about our dilemma because we wanted to spare them worry.

I was so lonely for my parents that winter. All three of

us kept up a strong front, but we missed them terribly. Every morning before walking to school, I pulled the shades down on the windows of the little cabin to help keep the warmth in. I also knew that if the shades were up when I got home, that would be a signal that Mom and Dad were there. I was usually the first to arrive at the end of the day. As I walked, my eyes would be focused ahead, ready for my first glimpse of our cabin. When it came into view, I looked anxiously to see if the shades were up.

One glorious day in April, the shades were up; when I saw this, my heart nearly burst with emotion. I started to cry, tears streaming down my face as I ran to the cabin. By the time I reached the front door, I was hit by the unmistakable smell of fresh bread in the oven. Mom sat in the rocker, crocheting. Sobbing, I ran to her and fell at her feet, wrapping my arms around her legs. As she stroked my hair and said my name over and over, I heard Dad coming up from the basement, which was a tricky endeavor with only half of a staircase. As his head cleared the top of the stairs, he spotted me in a heap on the floor and said, "Audrey, what in the blankety-blank happened to the stairs and the furniture?"

I explained the story of the woodcutters' strike and how we were freezing. Mom and Dad had no idea what we had experienced during the winter. As Mom fixed tea, I detailed the trying months, and my dad's countenance quickly softened. The young man's inheritance was smaller, but the Purkeypile children were alive and safe.

To have Mom and Dad with us in the cabin produced the most wonderful feeling—instantly we moved from merely existing to being warm, cozy, and secure. How does that happen? The three of us were thrilled beyond description. I cried for days.

Mom, Dad, and Gramps left Poorman in 1943 because there was no longer any mining production in the camp. Dad bought a home on the same street as our little rental cabin facing the Chena River. I graduated from Fairbanks High School in May 1944 in a graduating class of seventeen students and made plans to attend college. World War II was in its fourth year, and June and I were active in the USO. Often, we traveled to dances on army aircraft. During one of the dances, June met a young G.I., whom she married in 1945.

When the war was in its latter stages, my mother wrote the following letter to her cousin Alice from Fairbanks on December 7, 1944.

Dear Alice,

Your nice letter has reached me at last. It went down to Poorman and lay there for a long time, until a trapper came by and carried it back to Ruby. Poorman is a dead town now. The only person there is an old man who is taking care of our place. After the war is over, we expect to go back, but for the present we have bought a house here and are settled until the big show is over.

Audrey won a scholarship to the University of Alaska and is attending there this winter. She wants to become a nurse.

We are all very much interested in hearing of your boys, Bud and Phil. [Note: Both boys were in the military service.] Every time we hear of the B29s, we think of Phil. Yes, we subscribe to Life Magazine and saw the picture of the plane. There is also one out here at Ladd Field for cold-weather testing. June and Irus have seen it.

Today is Pearl Harbor Day, and our B29s were

over Tokyo trying to even the score. You folks are surely carrying your share of this war's burden.

We are all wondering what will happen to our Alaska after the war. It looks as though the Pioneer Days are over. The army and war work have changed the whole face of the land.

Love and best wishes to you all from all of us.

Your cousin,

Ciss

My mother wrote to her cousin again less than one month later. She had received word that Alice's son Phil was missing in action.

January 5, 1945

Dear Alice,

Your letter reached us on Christmas Eve. Ever since, our hearts have gone out to you all in love and sympathy. When our first boy was taken away from us, it was as though the sun had darkened for a long time. Irus Jr. was only an infant, so I know your loss is increased a hundredfold because Phil has been with you so much longer. We will all join you in praying to God that he may yet be found and restored to you. It will be a hard, trying time for you, and God alone can give the strength to bear. Words seem empty, Alice, dear, but our hearts and prayers are with you. Let us know as soon as you hear of Phil. Irus was reading of a B29 crew coming in somewhere after being lost. We were so hoping it was Phil and his men.

Your loving cousin,

Ciss

In December 1945, my mother wrote:

> *Dear Alice,*
> *Irus and I are thinking of you and Frank. This Christmas, when people are rejoicing, your hearts are sore and sad. Our thoughts and love are with you.*
> *Your cousin,*
> *Ciss*

Step by step...Sometimes we move forward in life step by step.

COLLEGE YEARS

At the age of seventeen, I started my first year of college at the University of Alaska at Fairbanks in the fall of 1944. At that time, almost all of the men were in the service, leaving only women or young men who were 4F (not qualified for military service due to medical reasons) on campus. Only about fifty students attended the university that year, but the school kept all of the teachers to maintain their accreditation. I had several pre-nursing classes and sometimes would be the only one in the class, so I received some excellent one-on-one instruction.

In the fall of 1945, I began my sophomore year of college at the University of Washington. Mom heard of a girl also going to Seattle named Margaret Prince. Her parents had recently moved to Fairbanks, so we met and made plans to travel to school together. Both of us stayed with Auntie Jennie until we decided to move on campus.

Although the war had officially ended, most of the young men remained on duty. Fraternities, in order to make their mortgage payments, began renting rooms to female students, so Margaret and I moved into the basement of a fraternity house along with five other nursing students.

That winter, Seattle had unusually cold weather. The fraternity heater did not work properly and there were no men around to fix it. History repeated itself. I am not certain if it was my idea, but it probably was. The girls and I went into the alley behind the fraternity and sawed down wooden clothesline poles to burn in the fireplace. The alley soon became void of clothesline poles, but we survived the winter.

For our protection, we had a midnight curfew. One day, friends from Fairbanks were in Seattle visiting and asked me to take them on a ferry boat ride. The boat would not return to shore until midnight, which would mean that I would miss curfew, but friends from home were important to me and I decided to go anyway. Returning from the ferry docks after midnight, I found the fraternity house locked up tight. My roommates had been watching for me and pulled me through the window. They quickly wound my hair around large pink curlers and stuffed me into the bunk, as if I had been asleep for hours. Within minutes, the house monitor arrived for the second bed check. The girl announced that I had not been there earlier and she had been looking for me. In spite of our insistence that I had been in bed the entire time, she turned me in and we were all called to talk to the council. One by one, my roommates were called into the council meeting and stated that I was in bed long before the curfew. Our story was believed and I was spared expulsion from school; however, there was a cost. More than sixty years later, I still regret lying to the council.

My years at the University of Washington were rewarding, and I worked very hard. An average semester schedule included twenty-one hours of mainly science and pre-medicine coursework. During our sophomore year, Margaret and I moved into a dormitory, and I worked every day in the cafeteria serving food. After my work shift, I raced up four flights of stairs, quickly changed into my uniform, put my hair up, and ran to the hospital. The forty dollars a month earned was a critical factor in keeping me in school. Dad sent me some money, but each school year cost close to fifteen hundred dollars, so working was essential. After completing my sophomore year in the spring of 1946, I was ready to go into the hospital for three years of nursing, but had lost weight and became very tired. Exhaustion turned to loneliness, and my thoughts continually turned toward home.

My brother, Dave, sent me some money to visit the family in Alaska, and I decided to stay there for a semester to rest. Following the end of the war, Mom, Dad, and Dave had returned to Poorman to reopen the Roadhouse, hoping that mining would again resume in the area.

The time in Poorman was a period of refreshment and renewal. Dave and I rebuilt a sled dog team and spent hours traveling to visit the surrounding mining camps. Each day, I arose early, setting out trap lines to snare ptarmigan, grouse, and rabbits. My biggest prize was the capture of two martens that I sold for one hundred dollars. Although I loved being back in Alaska with the family, I was determined to complete my nursing degree and returned to Washington in January 1947.

The prize martens.

Margaret and I lived in a dormitory with several girls in the nursing program, and we became known as the "Basic 33." We would be the 33rd class of nursing students to graduate from the University of Washington. Ten of us became very close, and we have continued to meet together once a decade. In 1999, we met in Seattle for our fiftieth reunion.

In August 1949, I graduated with a B.S. in Nursing.

The day of graduation, a courier came with a corsage and a note from my mom. Her note stated how sorry she was that she could not come to the graduation. She was very proud of her daughter. I was the only graduate wearing a corsage that day.

Nurse Audrey at the University of Washington.

After graduation, I worked at Harbor View Hospital for several months before returning to Fairbanks to work in a clinic. Mom and Dad flew down to Seattle, and together we drove back to Fairbanks on the Alcan Highway. I had the grand idea of joining the navy and being stationed in Hawaii. The thought of warmth and palm trees and sandy beaches was appealing. Plus, I would not have to burn furniture to stay warm in Hawaii. But my dream of life on a tropical island was not meant to be. As my mom's early plans to go to China changed when she fell in love with Dad, I happily gave up my independent plans when I met my husband-to-be, John Wilcox.

LIFE BEYOND ALASKA

BACK IN FAIRBANKS, I LIVED TEMPORARILY WITH MY SIS-ter Mimi and her family while working in a medical clinic. Missing university social life, I began attending the Sunday evening college class at the Presbyterian Church and met several lonely young service men. One young man called me to see if I wanted to go on a double date. Unaware of his ulterior motive, I agreed. He had seen me with my friend Molly, a Scottish girl, and developed a plan to meet her. Prior to our date, Don called me. "Audrey, I'm short and my friend is quite tall. Would you mind going with my friend and I will go with Molly?" (Molly was a mere five feet tall.)

My blind date with John Wilcox, the tall air force staff sergeant from Larned, Kansas, established the direction of the rest of my life. We dated for eight months and were married on Valentine's Day, February 14, 1951. Our children have all been amused that the little white Presbyterian Church where we said our vows now resides in the Alaskaland Museum in Fairbanks, Alaska.

In 1952, following a brief stay in Washington, we loaded all of our belongings, including our baby daughter, into our 1947 Pontiac convertible and moved to Kansas, where John completed his engineering degree at the University of Kansas. Having never been outside of Alaska, Canada, or Seattle, I was not sure what to make of Kansas, but fifty-six years later we remain in the Midwest. Four children plus spouses, eleven grandchildren (plus four spouses), and four great-grandchildren later...our lives are full and blessed.

> *In 1904, I left Seattle for Nome to make a fortune; found not much gold, but a wife and later five children—gosh—struck it rich after all, I guess.*
> —*Irus W. Purkeypile*

My parents lived the rest of their days in Alaska, California, and Washington. In 1960, one year after Alaska became a state, they were honored by the Pioneers of Alaska at the annual Golden Days Festival. Crowned King and Queen Regent in Fairbanks, my parents were recognized for their significant contributions to Alaska and its people.

In 1987, my sisters, brother, and I visited Selawik together. Fifty years after leaving the village, the trip resembled a pilgrimage back to the place of our youth. As usual, Mimi was the driving force behind the plans. She had not been to Selawik since 1934 when, at the age of fourteen, she left from Kotzebue to attend school in Seattle. Emotions were high when our airplane flew over the village and landed downriver from Selawik. After arriving at the airstrip, the five of us were rowed in small boats on the river to the site where our schoolhouse once stood. As we scrambled up the bank, all of us were transported back more than fifty years to the hundreds of times we had felt this land under our feet. Alerted to our plans to visit, the villagers were expecting us, and several of our childhood playmates had planned a luncheon. "You were my babies!" The voice was unmistakable. One of our nannies, Esther, had traveled from Kotzebue to greet us.

Much had changed in our village. Wooden walkways lined the banks of the river where our dirt paths had been carved. A walking bridge connecting three sections of Selawik spanned the river. Although the bell from our schoolhouse had been preserved, the building had been replaced with a new school. Next to the school, a shower house and laundry provided a service for those still without plumbing; many of the Selawik residents remained in one-room cabins.

The Purkeypile siblings in Selawik, 1987, standing under the original school bell from their school.

Lucy, the Eskimo woman who fed me ice cream made from snow, seal oil, and berries, still lived in Selawik, and I was able to visit her home. Her cabin had been enlarged but was in the same location—across the river from our schoolhouse site. After our family moved to Poorman, Lucy had a daughter whom she named Audrey. This daughter had died several years before my visit. After showing me to a chair, the sweet woman said, "Just a minute, Audrey. I have something for you." She left for another room, soon reappearing and holding a watch. "This watch belonged to my daughter, Audrey. I always knew you would come back, so I saved it for you." I treasure the watch to this day.

Our nanny, Esther, invited us to visit her home in Kotzebue before leaving the area. While there, June and I walked to the local hospital to see Viola's mother, Rosie Foster. Although Mrs. Foster had suffered a stroke and could not speak, her face broke into a joyful smile when we entered the room. After fifty years, she knew us immediately. I was her young daughter's best friend, and this mother had not forgotten me. This is the way of the people of Alaska; community and lifelong commitment to one another are as important as the air they breathe.

Sometimes we want it all back—the simplicity, the laughter, the warmth and comfort of other days. We want it back, but know that it will never be the same. My childhood was magical. Despite the bitter cold, we always felt warmth. Despite the danger, we always felt safe. Despite the complications involved with merely surviving, our lives were simple.

Memories of my childhood enable me to hold on to the things that I love and to know who I am today. I never want to lose the memories. As I grow older, the dates might fade, but the moments will never grow dim. The places, the people, and the moments we shared will be with me forever.

EPILOGUE

"HELLO, MY DEAR CHERYL GIRL." GRAM ALWAYS CALLED me Cheryl Girl. Her voice was soft and sweet with an unmistakable Canadian accent. Everything about my Gram was nurturing and mild-mannered. Her touch was gentle and kind. The calico dress and apron on her petite body were predictable—I never saw her in anything else. A lace handkerchief with embroidered purple pansies in one corner was tucked into the pocket of her apron. My Gram could always be found in one of two places—the kitchen or in her rocking chair, a handmade afghan across her knees. She had meticulously crocheted and bound multicolored squares to create a size perfect for her lap. I always wanted her to tell me stories about Alaska; she always wanted to know how I was doing in school.

"Ouch, Grandad! You're scratchy!" Sometimes when he hugged me tight, the rough, prickly stubble on his face pressed hard against my cheek and I thought my ribs would surely crack. He was always warm—or maybe his hug was warm. Or maybe it was my body pressing close to his plaid flannel shirt, complete with suspenders. The smell of pipe tobacco was strong and I breathed it in, turning this distinct aroma into a memory. Grandad's fingers, yellowed from years of stuffing the pipe with the pungent tobacco leaves, would grip my shoulders as he held me out and said, "Let me get a good look at you and see how much you have grown!"

Grandad died in November 1969, at the age of eighty-six. While living in Port Angeles, Washington, he fell into a coma following a stroke. The decision was made to take him back to his beloved Alaska. My mother, Nurse Audrey, accompanied her parents on the long airplane ride to Fairbanks. Although locked in deep unconsciousness, my grandfather's face lit up and his lips curved upward into a brilliant smile as he was carried off the plane onto Alaskan soil. He was home.

Five months following my grandfather's death, my grandmother died peacefully at my Aunt Mimi's home in California. After fifty years of marriage and an extraordinary partnership, man and wife were together again.

My mother, Audrey, has suffered the loss of not only her parents, but of her three sisters, Mimi, Norma, and June. David lives in Fairbanks. Like their parents, all have been recognized as true pioneers of Alaska.

What I learned from my grandparents is this: Not all of life is lived in the times when the water runs. They consistently lived life with grace and purpose during the unwanted seasons of darkness and isolation as well as those joyful seasons of light and refreshment. This is the legacy left by my grandparents, Irus and Sara Purkeypile. This will be the legacy that Audrey Purkeypile Wilcox will leave to her children and grandchildren and generations to come.

Through their relationship with my mother, my family has seen abundant evidence of the pioneer spirit. Often, we are amused when observing things she does. My mother does not realize that at the age of eighty she probably should not be clearing tree limbs from the roads in her community or hauling rocks to help a neighbor landscape. One only has to mention the name "Audrey" to draw a smile from the hearer.

My mother's life has been driven by the things that are important. She understands the value of hard work and embraces it, as if she has something to contribute that is necessary for survival. My mother has always been one who prepares and plans, staying very busy, but making time for people. She continues to minister to others daily by teaching Bible studies, visiting shut-ins, sitting with those in the hospital, and volunteering for numerous organizations.

My mother can be described as a positive person with a "can do" attitude and an ability to rebound. She has confidence in the future and a longer, broader view of life—things will get better, things will work out. Within days of undergoing cancer surgery, she received a visit from a woman who pulled a chair up next to the bed and shared that *she* had just been diagnosed with cancer. Although in pain herself, my mother spent the next hour comforting this friend and assuring her that the sun will again shine and the water will indeed run again.

While on this book-writing journey, I have come to know my grandparents in a way that has enriched my life and has given me new understanding and appreciation of Alaska and its people. On this journey, I have come to more fully appreciate my mother, her strength, her character, and her pioneer spirit. May my journey never end.

Sara rejoicing in the time when the water runs